SALEM

The story of the Baptist Church in Biggin Street and Maison Dieu Road, Dover, and its associated chapels

BY
PAMELA GODDEN

Pamela Godden

Copyright © Pamela Godden 2001

The right of Pamela Godden to be identified as the author of this work has been asserted by her in accordance with the Copyright, Designs and Patents Act 1988

ISBN 0-9541977-0-4

Published by Dover Baptist Church, 27–32 Maison Dieu Road, Dover, Kent CT16 1RF

Printed in England by A R Adams & Son (Printers) Ltd, Dour Street, Dover, Kent

Design AEP

Contents

Preface / *page 5*

Acknowledgements / *page 7*

CHAPTER 1   Origins / *page 9*

CHAPTER 2   Men and ministries / *page 17*

CHAPTER 3   Buildings / *page 64*

CHAPTER 4   Church organisation, association and worship / *page 80*

CHAPTER 5   Salem's associated chapels / *page 95*

CHAPTER 6   Youth / *page 109*

CHAPTER 7   Loving our neighbours / *page 122*

CHAPTER 8   Mission / *page 131*

CHAPTER 9   Past and future / *page 144*

APPENDIX   Church Statistics / *page 149*

Bibliography / *page 153*

Index / *page 155*

This book is dedicated to
Nigel Booth
whose outstanding ministry at
Salem was cut short on
28th March 2002
just two weeks before publication.

Preface

This book is written to tell the story of the church's first hundred and sixty two years to its members and friends. In order to keep it reasonably short and interesting I have used a narrative form, but I am conscious that in order to do so I may sometimes have over-simplified the complex reality. Information on dates, places and events is as accurate as I can make it; comments on personalities, motives and relationships depend on my interpretation of the available data, and to those on earth and in heaven who read and cry, 'No, it wasn't like that at all', I apologise and admit that I may be mistaken. For anyone who would like more detail, notes and references are available from the church on request. I have also tried to avoid overloading the book with names which will mean nothing to many readers, but lists of members and church officers for most periods are available to anyone interested.

Thanks are due to many people who helped to make the book what it is, including all those who shared memories and provided pictures. In particular I would like to record my thanks to Geoffrey Breed, the Kent Baptist Association's archivist, and to Trish Godfrey from the local studies section of Dover Public Library, both of whom answered patiently my endless questions and pointed me in the direction of further information, to my daughters for the use of their computer in preparing the manuscript, to Arthur Pallet for his extensive work in making it ready for the printer, and to Nigel Booth for the original idea and for all his subsequent interest and encouragement.

P. Godden 2001

Acknowledgements

Acknowledgements are given to Dover Museum for the pictures on pages 14, 23 and 70 and to Dover Express for the picture on page 107. Unless otherwise stated, quotations in the text are from the church meeting minutes or from the church's annual letter to the local association.

... Said Chapel or Meetinghouse and Premises to be used as a place of public religious worship by the Christian Church now meeting for Divine Worship therein and maintaining the Doctrines of the Deity and Atonement of our Lord Jesus Christ, the Divine Influences of the Holy Spirit and Justification by Faith in our Lord Jesus Christ ... and ... to permit to officiate in the said Meetinghouse ... such person or persons of unblamable moral character maintaining the Doctrines aforesaid and practising Baptism by Immersion to such persons only as are of years of understanding upon their own confession of repentance towards God and faith in and obedience to our Lord Jesus Christ, as three fourths of the Members of the said Society (Female as well as Male) ... elect as their Minister or Pastor therein.

(extract from trust deeds of the chapel)

CHAPTER 1

Origins

THE Christian Church began its life at Pentecost in the year of the crucifixion of Jesus Christ. This was when the men and women who had been with Jesus during his life and had seen him die and seen him risen again, were transformed from a doubtful, fearful bunch of would-be followers into The Believers, who would from then on live a new life and preach a new message.

From the beginning it was a group of people who believed that Jesus had come to bring God's love and message to men, had been put to death on a cross and had risen from the dead by God's power. From the beginning they claimed that God was working in them by a particular power, the power of the Holy Spirit, and in that power they lived, shared belongings and worship, prayed together, sustained each other in persecution, ate meals together in memory of Christ's death, and looked forward to the day when the world would end and He would come again.

But it was not all plain sailing. The ways of God are too high and too complex for men to understand fully, and the devil is always ready to push any particular doctrine farther than it can properly go and to stir up controversy between those who hold one side of an argument and those who hold the other. Within a very short time people trying to puzzle out exactly what the faith meant came to different conclusions. Over the centuries the Church has been divided on whether Jesus always had the divine nature or whether he gained it at his baptism, on what exactly happens when people take the bread and the wine, on whether everyone may be saved or only those God has previously chosen, on whether the Bible is to be taken literally at all points,

Chapter 1

and on many other issues – all of which may appear abstract and theoretical to outsiders but which if seriously considered can have a very real impact on how the Church lives and worships and how it relates to the world beyond its walls. In twenty centuries of Christianity the one Church has become many churches, all with their own customs, creeds and doctrines - though by God's grace in spite of everything they are still one in the essentials, still the Body of Christ on earth, doing their best to live His life and fulfil His commands.

One of the greatest breaks between the branches of the church came in the sixteenth century. The Roman Catholic church at that time was in a bad way. It had been the State church and almost the only church in Europe for a thousand years, and without opposition it had become flabby. Once you had been baptised as a baby you were part of the Church, and from then on the Church would carry you without any great effort on your behalf. All you needed to do was to go to Mass now and then to hear the priest interceding for you - and if your life wasn't as good as it might have been, your relations could pay a sum of money to the Church after your death to buy forgiveness for you. The laity had no need of faith or prayer or sanctity. Many of the clergy were ignorant, even illiterate, and often far from holy themselves. The devil, no doubt, was rubbing his hands with satisfaction.

But in Wittenberg in Germany in 1520 there lived a priest called Martin Luther, who found that the practices of the Church of Rome did not help him to know forgiveness or peace with God. In Paul's letter to the Romans he read that forgiveness depended on believing that Jesus died to save him, and that once forgiven a person can live a new and holy life through His Spirit, and he felt, he said, as if he had been born anew and entered through open gates into Paradise itself. After spending much time thinking the matter through he wrote out ninety-five points of difference between this New Testament view and that of the Catholic Church and nailed them to the Cathedral door in Wittenberg. The Reformation was born.

Many changes came out of the Reformation, secular as well as ecclesiastical. It contributed to the Renaissance view of man and his place in the universe, which brought new perspectives in art and science and medicine. In England

Henry VIII rejected the authority of the Pope, divorced his wife and proclaimed a new state church, the Church of England, with himself as its head. The Roman Catholic church itself was shaken up and forced to rethink some of its traditions, and it did so with some success, but by then it had lost its total supremacy over the people of Europe. New communitites of believers were formed and grew and developed, proclaiming a faith that was based not on centuries of tradition but directly on Bible teaching.

The Church had not so much cracked in two at the Reformation as splintered into many pieces. These new churches, having begun to question, went on questioning, and as time went on they moved apart not only from the Catholics but from each other. They differed in the organisation of the local church and the form of worship, in who they admitted to membership and how they admitted them, in how they took communion and what they believed about it, in how they related to the state, and on many other points. They called themselves Lutherans, Calvinists, Presbyterians, Independents.

One of the more disputed of the new beliefs concerned baptism. It was not true, insisted many of the new Protestants, that a baby could be made a member of the Church by baptism before it could even speak. This was quite contrary to New Testament teaching and practice, because baptism should be a sign that a person believed in Jesus Christ, and how could a baby be said to believe? Infant baptism had no meaning, they said, and if a person wanted to be a true member of the church he must be baptised when he was old enough to think for himself. Since virtually every child at that time had already been baptised as an infant, these people were called 'anabaptists', or re-baptisers, and all anabaptists gained a bad name when one group, who also held other extreme views, took over the town of Münster in Westphalia and were not defeated until the army beseiged the town and eventually put them all to death. The name Baptists persisted, however, and was given to two particular groups of Christians for whom believers' baptism was a central tenet of their belief.

The Particular Baptists followed John Calvin in claiming that only a certain number of people would be saved. They drew from such passages as Romans 8: 29–30 the belief that God had chosen particular people for eternal life, and

Chapter 1

that only those he had chosen would be saved. There were Particular Baptist churches in Kent from the seventeenth century.

The General Baptists, on the other hand, though they shared many of the Particular Baptists' beliefs – in particular of course the insistence on believers' baptism – insisted that anyone who trusted in the redeeming death of Christ would be saved. They began in Lincolnshire, left England in 1608 because of persecution and went to live in Amsterdam. When the persecution had died away a group returned and formed churches particularly in Kent and other counties of Southern England. There was a General Baptist Church meeting in Dover at least from the early 1640s, and others about that time in Biddenden, Chatham and Tunbridge Wells.

The early history of the Dover church is full of dramatic episodes. Between 1661 and 1689 it was illegal in England to hold any religious meeting of more than five people unless it was an Anglican service using the Book of Common Prayer. Ministers who had taken such a dissenting meeting were banished five miles from where it had been held, and those who attended one could be fined or sent to gaol. If anyone couldn't pay the fine his posessions could be sold to cover it – and if that still wasn't enough the possessions of other members of the congregation could be sold to make up the shortfall. But the Dover Baptists were firm in their convictions: they flouted the law and were duly fined. Meetings of more than a hundred Dissenters were not unknown, with some of the influential men of the town present. On one occasion an Army Captain was sent to listen from behind the bushes to one such open-air meeting, hoping to hear them convict themselves. Instead of arresting them, however, he was himself converted as he listened. His name was Samuel Tavernor, and he later became the pastor of the church, which met for some years in his house in Market Lane (now vanished). On a later occasion he was himself arrested and imprisoned in Dover Castle. In 1671 the Law ordered that the pulpits and benches of the Dover Baptists should be broken down and the doors of the meeting house fastened with padlocks - but on the following Sunday morning it is recorded that the doors were broken open and the service held as usual. The church held out until the Toleration Act was passed in 1689, and when Samuel Tavernor returned

> '
> Enclosed within a valiant captain lies
> Holy and humble, pious, grave and wise,
> A Gospel pastor faithful to his trust '
> Expecting to be raised with the just.
>
> *(Inscription on Samuel Tavernor s gravestone)* [originally in St Martin s burial ground in Princes Street. Died 1696. From *Dover Express* 23rd January 1970]

from London, where he had escaped, the south-west end of his house was licensed as a place of religious worship. In 1745 the first actual chapel was built, further along Market Lane.

The church continued meeting through the eighteenth century, with rather less drama now that the official persecution was over. But in the early nineteenth century many of the country's General Baptists made another of those shifts which changed the whole focus of the church. They began to move towards the view that God is not Three-in-One, but only One, that the Son and the Holy Spirit are inferior to God the Father – a doctrine that was to be called Unitarianism and was not fully Christian. The General Baptist Church in Dover was one that made this change, and by the time they built their new chapel off Adrian Street in 1820 they were no longer really Baptists at all, though they called themselves Unitarian General Baptists for a while longer before eventually dropping the name 'Baptist' altogether. At much about the same time the church at Eythorne, which had been meeting continuously since its early days and at this point called itself a Particular Baptist, received a request from sixteen members who worshipped there but lived in Dover. Could they leave the mother church and begin a new church in Dover, so that the Baptist cause in Dover would not be lost? The church at Eythorne duly dismissed them, only regretting that they would be lost to the Eythorne fellowship, and the local association gave them £60 to begin

Chapter 1

*Pentside chapel, seen behind a ship in Wellington Dock
(photo courtesy of Dover Museum)*

the work. They held their first meetings in a chemist's shop in Snargate Street in 1821.

At first the new church in Dover seems to have flourished. By 1823 they were able to buy a site on the quayside overlooking what is now Wellington Dock and build a chapel there, which they called Pentside chapel. They had two ministers with short-lived pastorates and then Rev. Daniel Crambrook came and stayed for eleven years. The congregation grew. By 1838 there were 139 members and 140 in the Sunday School. But in 1839 a new schism arose. Sixteen of Pentside's members were unhappy there, and they in turn asked to be dismissed so that they could begin afresh as a separate Church somewhere else.

This time the break was anything but amicable. The exact form of the dispute is lost in the mists of time, but part of the problem was the question whether any Christian should be allowed to take communion in that church, or whether it should be restricted to baptised members. Some of the congregation, too, objected when an unordained person was allowed to preside at communion. There were strong personalities involved, and both sides, of course, were sure that they were in the right. What may have begun quietly soon swelled into a volcano of criticism and counter-criticism. Intemperate allegations were made on both sides. Phrases were used like 'accusations injurious to character' and 'contrary to propriety and decorum and the letter and spirit of Christianity'. Attempts to settle the matter amicably failed. A motion was made, and sanctioned by all but one of the deacons, to suspend the rebellious members. They in turn made the sweeping indictment that the Church as constituted then 'renders it impossible for order – union – usefulness or peace'.

So the sixteen drafted a letter asking the Church to release them. It was not a document calculated to appease, listing their grievances without much apology and finishing with references to 'every unkind act' and a prayer that God would give those they left behind repentance and purity as well as blessing.

Perhaps understandably, the Pentside Church did not receive this letter kindly. The dispute was taken to the East Kent Baptist Association, who were asked to come and arbitrate. They came as requested and listened to both sides, and though they felt that the aggrieved members had a certain amount of justification for their request they recommended that that letter with its inflammatory phrasing should be withdrawn and another should be sent, couched in more general terms. Then, they said, they would recommend that the dismissal should be granted.

This was not the end of the struggle. Further letters were sent, lost, rejected, amended and sent again. Pentside would not easily agree to a dismissal that made it appear that they were at fault. But in the end it became obvious that the rebels were not going to give in, and in April 1839 they at last agreed to let them go.

The dispute could not have been the best of witnesses to the town. Did people wonder that the God of peace could not even reconcile his own flock to one another? But Dover was growing fast, and there were more than enough citizens to supply two congregations. Though the new Church was born out of conflict, it was able to settle down and organise itself peaceably

Chapter 1

once it was allowed. Both churches were to grow over the years into strong, evangelical bodies. If the devil thought that having divided he was well on the way to conquering them entirely, he was to be disillusioned. God could use the new church as well as the old to speak to those he wanted to call to Himself.

So on 22nd April 1839 the sixteen ex-Pentside members met for the first time officially in William Corbett's schoolroom on Military Road, and the new church was formed. Within a year they were to build a chapel for themselves, and to call it Salem.

CHAPTER 2

Men and ministries

A CHURCH needs a leader. The men and women who became the new church were a strong body of people who knew their own mind, but as soon as they had settled formally in Military Road they began to consider who they would call as their minister.

They found a man whose wise counsel did much to guide and strengthen the young church, a man called James P. Hewlett. He had been trained at Bradford College, Yorkshire and had spent four years as the minister at Kingsbridge in Devon, and it was there that they wrote to him in May 1839. They wanted, they said, a faithful and zealous minister of Jesus Christ to work among them. He had relations in the area and had taken services in Dover before, and his services were 'so generally acceptable' that they were inviting him to come, for three months at first, to labour in the cause of Jesus Christ among them. They could only pledge to support him to the tune of £100 a year – not much more than the wage of a factory foreman – but they hoped that after a few years they would be able to increase this.

He accepted the call (though he rejected the three months' trial period), and his recognition service took place in October 1839 at the Wesleyan Chapel in Snargate Street. It was still a small church that he began to lead. Church meetings that first year in the schoolroom were only the size of deacons' meetings today. But there was a spirit of eagerness and enthusiasm, and the numbers were already beginning to increase. Some people were transferring their membership from other churches, and some were newly converted and wanting to be baptised. There was no baptistry in the

Chapter 2

schoolroom, of course, and they made an attempt to patch up relations with Pentside by asking them for the use of theirs.

But they weren't going to need another church's baptistry for long. Even before Hewlett was invited to the pastorate a building committee had been set up. They had no money to speak of, but that did not deter them. At first they bought a piece of land in Russell Street for £300, and started planning to build. Then they had second thoughts. That plot was too small, too near the Independent chapel and too far from where they were meeting in Military Road. (That is what is recorded. Perhaps it was also in their mind that they would be wise to build farther up the town, in a different area from Pentside and drawing on a different population.) So they bought another plot, for 1000 guineas, this time in Biggin Street, and on April 20th 1840 the foundation stone of the new chapel was laid.

In the meantime they were holding prayer meetings, Bible study, morning and evening services on Sundays and Sunday school, and the numbers were steadily growing. They were too many for the little schoolroom before the new chapel was built.

It was not all plain sailing, though, even in that first year. The question of communion arose again – a question which at that time was exercising wiser heads than theirs. Should they admit any Christian to communion (open communion), or limit it to members of their own church, or at least to those who had been baptised as adults (closed communion)? It was difficult because it touched on the much deeper and thornier questions of what made a person a Christian and how a Christian might be recognised. Painfully they hammered out a rule. Adult baptism, they decided, was very important, but not absolutely essential. They insisted that any minister they called must have been baptised as a believer, but ordinary members need not. Anyone who professed belief in Jesus Christ and walked with him might be a member of the church and take communion. This rule was agreed by a majority of the church meeting but not all, and one of the founder members, George Pearce, disagreed so strongly that he resigned his membership.

There was also the question of the gown. Some Baptist ministers wore the long plain 'Geneva' gown in the pulpit, but some felt that this was affected, and preached in ordinary clothes. It seemed to some of the congregation that their minister would be more respected if he wore the gown, and this too was a subject for heated debate, but this time they decided that the question was not of critical spiritual importance, and it was left to Hewlett's own discretion.

Rev James P. Hewlett

The chapel in Biggin Street was opened in August 1840. It would seat between four and five hundred people, and by the end of the second year of the church's existence it was well filled. They held three services on Sundays, and average congregations were 120 in the morning, 80 in the afternoon, and nearly 200 in the evening. During the week they had 50 at the week-night 'lecture' and 40 at the prayer meeting.

This was, of course, the period when church-going was the respectable thing to do on a Sunday. In less than a decade a census would show that fifty per cent of the nation's adults had attended a place of worship the previous Sunday (and Christian people were horrified at how low the figure was.) Perhaps the week-night figures are more representative of the real Christian witness among them. Nonetheless, allowing for age, illness and other responsibilities that is a very respectable number for a young church. Many a Baptist minister in England today would be speechless with joy to see forty people at the prayer-meeting every week.

The church members were very satisfied with Hewlett's ministry among them. 'Our eyes behold our teacher,' they said, 'And our ears hear the voice which says, "This is the way, walk ye in it".' They were all the more upset, then, when a London church wrote to him in 1842 and tried to persuade him to leave Dover, and duly relieved and grateful when 'out of pure love to the infant cause at Salem' he refused the offer.

He was to stay, in fact, for eight more years. They were good years, with the church growing and learning and reaching out to the community. More members were added, some by transfer, some by profession and baptism. Some also left Dover, or left Salem to join other churches, but overall the numbers increased. A Tract Distribution Society was formed, and a Christian Instruction Society. The Sunday School flourished, and two mission stations were established. In 1843 the East Kent Association of Particular Baptists held its annual meeting at Salem.

There were also griefs. In those days of limited medical knowlege death was a familiar visitor. The church told in their association letter that same year how a young man who had only just been baptised took communion for the first time one Sunday, was taken ill during the week and was dead within ten days. The church took consolation in the knowlege that he was now with his Lord, and were thrilled when someone who listened to a funeral sermon was thereby converted. Others were lost in other ways. The church required a godly lifestyle from its members, and more than one was excluded

---

Trustees of Salem 1840

Alfred Kingsford *brewer*
Edward Hills *coachmaker*
William Holtum Junr *tailor*
Thomas William Nowers *grocer*
William Phillips *shoemaker*
George Leach *bricklayer*
John Pearce *shoemaker*
Joseph Leonard Crowe *shoemaker*
Charles Collier *printer*
Theophilus Peter Hewlett *schoolmaster*
George Eliot Sargent *gentleman*
William Stanger *miller*

(Trust Deed Salem Chapel 1847. Minute Book 2 p75)

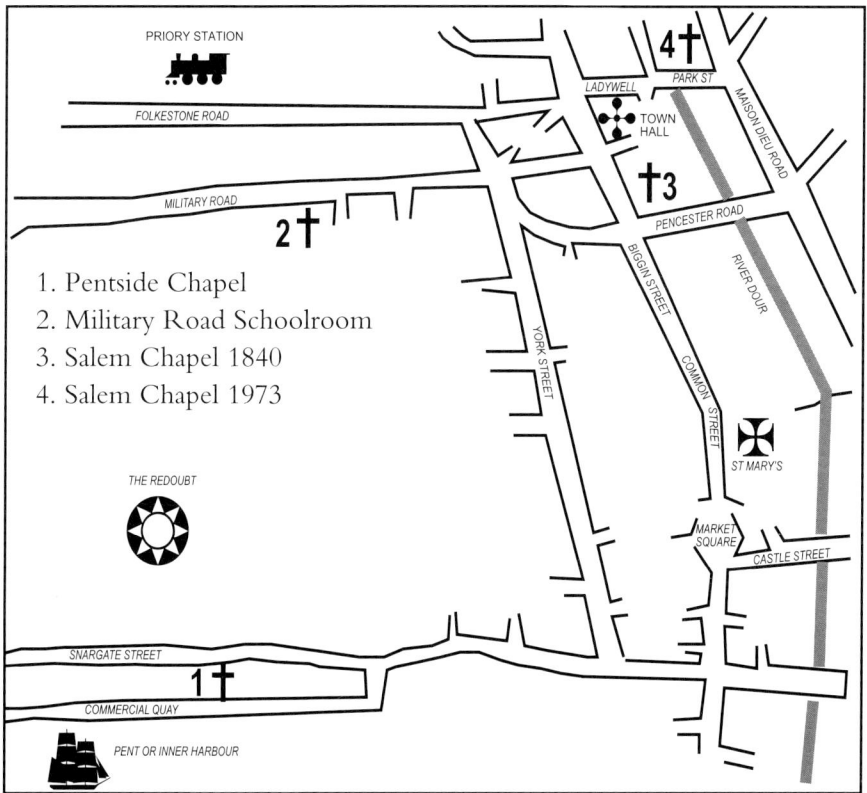

Note. The town of Dover has changed considerably since 1823. Some roads have been enlarged and junctions altered. Other roads, like Commercial Quay, have disappeared. This map is an amalgam of the old and the new and is intended just to help locate the church's various meeting places.

for immorality. The issue of a brother Hudson who was accused of dishonesty, and the dispute over whether he had really left Dover in order to escape from his creditors, rumbles through the minutes for several years. But over all the church flourished and grew strong, and in less than a decade the membership rose from 16 to 140.

Chapter 2

> '*All ecclesiastical bodies which are not useful are positively mischievous.*' *(Letter resigning from the Association 1848)*

So it must have come as something of a shock to hear in 1849 that Hewlett was intending to leave them. They had been planning a celebration of his ten years' ministry with them, and discovered sadly that the service would have to 'assume a valedictory form'. There is no reason given in the records for his departure. There had been financial problems for some years, and several attempts had been made to come to grips with them, apparently without lasting success. Then the question of the gown had come up again, but that had been settled without too much controversy. Probably Hewlett simply felt that he had given a good start to the young church and now God was calling him to work elsewhere. The valedictory service was held in December 1849 and he moved away to a pastorate at Watford.

So the church was thrown back for a while on its own resources. It was no longer the tiny body of men and women that had begun the work in 1839, but a good-sized group of people from varying walks of life. Several of the members were solid business-men – one of the deacons, William Pepper, for instance, and the treasurer, Alfred Kingsford. These two had been among the founder members, and with their families might reasonably be called pillars of the church. Alfred Kingsford owned and ran the Buckland Brewery, one of several small independent breweries in Dover at that time, which stood at the junction of Union (now Coombe Valley) Road and London Road. He was perhaps the wealthiest of the church members, and in 1846 he had accepted £1000 from the church and paid off the £1800 mortgage on the chapel, thus contributing £800 to its building. Pepper was a name well known in Dover. Several Peppers have been mayors in their time. William Pepper had taken the chair at the early meetings, and it may be his neat slanting copperplate that records the first minutes. For the rest, the church was a mixture of craftsmen and shopkeepers, labourers, employees, nurses and domestic servants. These now looked to God for guidance and began to consider the calling of

Men and Ministries

Alfred Kingsford's brewery in 1847 (Picture courtesy of Dover Museum)

Rev Frederic Bosworth

a new pastor.

The man they found was Frederic Bosworth, who was born in Cambridge but had trained at Montreal university and spent his first nine years of ministry in Canada. He was a classical scholar and the only M.A. Salem has ever had as minister. In 1850 he was staying in Dover and was asked to take services during the interregnum. He seems to have been a natural teacher. He asked if he could also start a course of Bible Classes during his stay, and both services and classes were received with so much enthusiasm that unanimously the church decided to invite him to remain and be their pastor.

He was thirty-seven years old when he began his ministry, and it appears that he was not in the

TEMPLE EWELL

ST MARGARET'S-A EWELL MINNIS

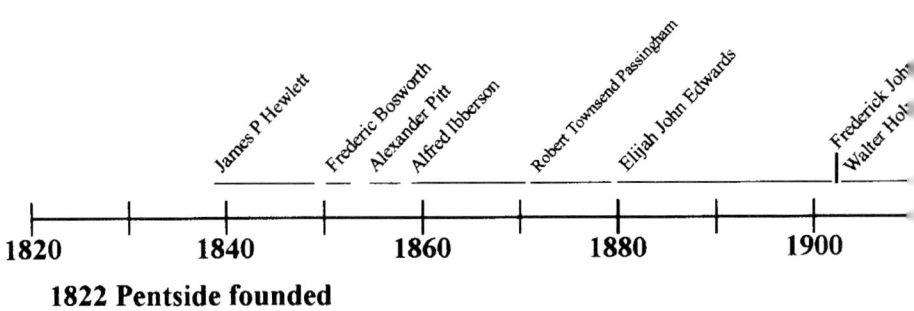

James P Hewlett
Frederic Bosworth
Alexander Pitt
Alfred Ibberson
Robert Townsend Passingham
Elijah John Edwards
Frederick John
Walter Hol

1820 — 1840 — 1860 — 1880 — 1900

1822 Pentside founded

SALEM
- Salem Chapel opened (Biggin Street)
- Graveyard closed
- New rooms built over school room
- Chapel enlarged
- Electric ligh

ACTIVITIES AT SALEM
Sunday School / Sunday Workshop
Dorcas Society
Missionary Society / Mission
Band of Hope
Christian Band
Total Abstine
Young P
B

*Diagram showing events in Salem's history.
The horizontal lines show the time-span of the chapels,
the ministries, and some of the activities that have taken
place at Salem. (Dates are approximate)*

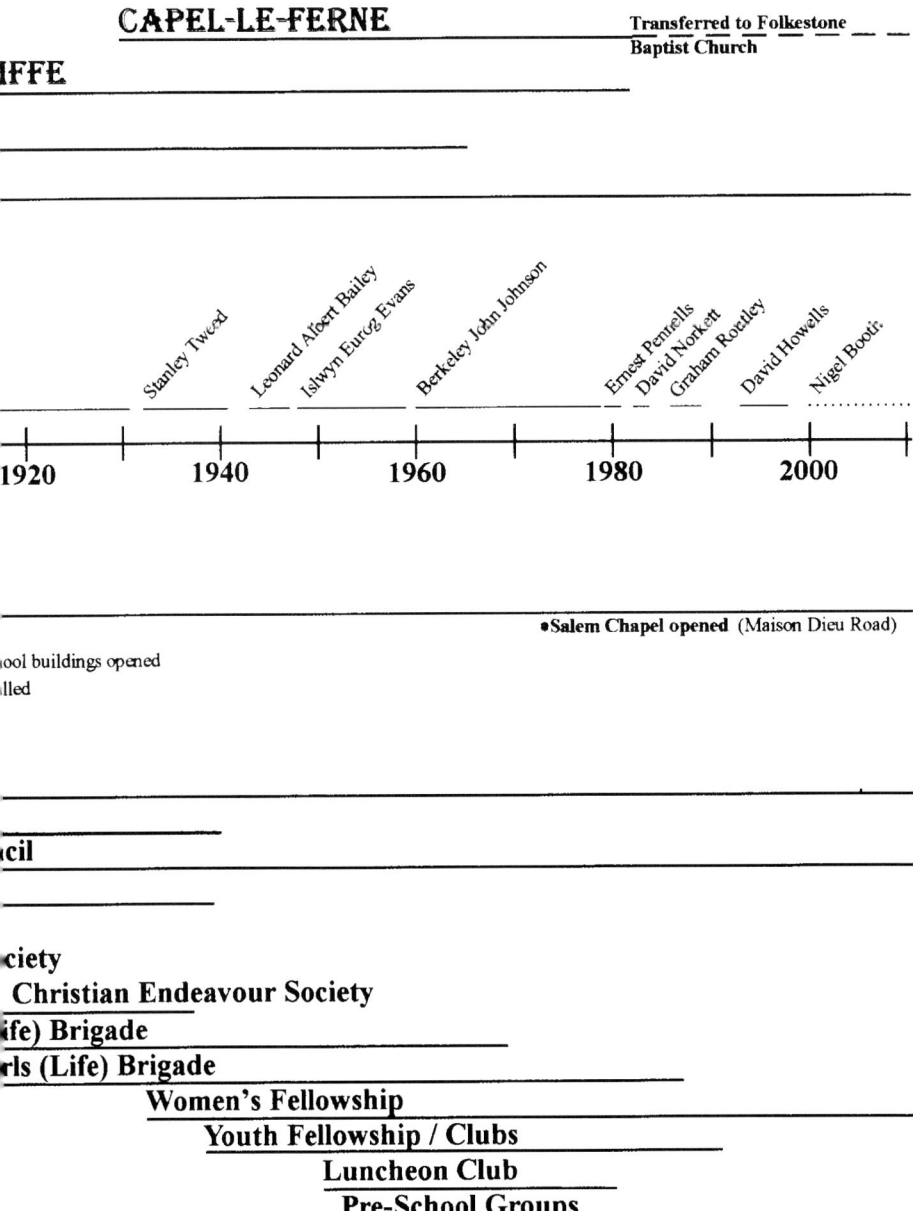

CAPEL-LE-FERNE

Transferred to Folkestone Baptist Church

IFFE

Stanley Tweed
Leonard Albert Bailey
Islwyn Eurog Evans
Berkeley John Johnson
Ernest Pennells
David Norkett
Graham Roadley
David Howells
Nigel Booth

1920   1940   1960   1980   2000

● **Salem Chapel opened** (Maison Dieu Road)

ool buildings opened
lled

cil

ciety
  Christian Endeavour Society
ife) Brigade
rls (Life) Brigade
        Women's Fellowship
          Youth Fellowship / Clubs
            Luncheon Club
              Pre-School Groups

Chapter 2

best of health. Perhaps he had been staying in Dover in the first place for the sake of its salubrious sea air. He was a quiet, reserved man; he was unmarried, and lodged with one of the church members in Norman Street. His was a fairly short ministry, not quite five years, and not a lot is known about it. It seems to have been the custom then for the chairman to write the minutes of the church meetings, which means writing them up after the meeting without detailed notes, and there is little in Bosworth's minutes of any interest. Those things which are recorded are mostly organisational, changes of the dates of church meetings, the acceptance or dismissal of members, and a resolution that only male members should be appointed as visitors to those applying for membership (no reason is given for this, which was a change from Salem's established practice.) But presumably the spiritual side of his ministry also flourished, for when he resigned in 1854 – to go to Bristol, where he would be minister at King Street Baptist church and also classical tutor at Bristol Baptist College – the church recorded their gratitude to God for their pastor's faithfulness and energy, his devoted labours and the holy consistency of his life. Alfred Kingsford, in fact, was so impressed that he called his son after him, and Frederic Bosworth Kingsford became deacon and treasurer in the church half a century later.

But after the smooth sailing of the first years, they were about to run into stormier waters. The church was no longer young and eager: it had established itself and now had to resist relaxing into a comfortable routine. To begin with, they became worried about the number of people who would not settle down and commit themselves to the church. They revised the whole roll, erasing those who no longer attended, or who had moved away from the town.

Then they had a little trouble finding a new pastor. Before, they had invited men who had accepted the invitation quickly. This time they had several months of interregnum. Five or six ministers preached for them on Sundays. One of these was invited to become their pastor, but declined. Another was considered, but the meeting was divided and they felt that it was necessary on so important a matter to have a unanimous vote. They turned to prayer, and stayed every Wednesday after the evening lecture for three-quarters of an hour to ask God's blessing on the labour to 'find a minister whom God would own and bless to the conversion of many souls'. Finally they met on an evening in October 1855, with the weather so bad that only thirty-four members were present out of a membership of 117, and they were not sure whether they should go ahead with so few. However, the motion to invite Alexander Pitt of Upton-on-Severn was carried unanimously by those who were there, and a letter was duly sent to him. He accepted.

Rev Alexander Pitt

He seems to have been a lively man with strong convictions, eloquent speech and plenty of ideas. During his ministry many came into the church, including one woman of nearly eighty, who 'rejoices to follow her Saviour's example in attending to the ordinance of baptism'. One young lady was first reminded of spiritual things at her brother's death-bed. Her father opposed her baptism because of her youth, the impressibility of her mind and her state of health; the church accepted her on profession of faith without baptism, but said that it was only her health that was relevant.

There were more practical matters, too. Enough money was raised to build a new schoolroom over the old one to house the growing Sunday School. Members were asked to make efforts to show strangers to pews and give them hymn-books. The church's library was overhauled.

But problems with money dogged the church all through Pitt's pastorate. He had requested a salary of £150, and maybe this was beyond the church's resources. Alfred Kingsford had resigned as treasurer in 1855 – though he remained a deacon – and perhaps they missed his wise counsel. At any rate money, or the lack of it, was a recurrent theme.

It was not usual at that time to depend on a voluntary offering at Sunday services for the church's work. Collections were sometimes taken – and Pitt suggested that notice should be given of these on the previous Sunday, presumably so that people could then put more cash than usual in the pockets of their Sunday suits. But most of the money came from pew rents – rent paid for the privilege of sitting regularly (or even not so regularly) in a particular pew – or from weekly subscriptions. Perhaps these subscriptions were not always paid, for a further plan was agreed that the whole church should be divided into districts and someone should go round to each house on Mondays collecting the money. The collectors were also encouraged to try to elicit subscriptions from non-members. But despite all these efforts money was short, and there was still a mortgage on the chapel to be paid off.

In 1856 they made a tremendous effort and raised £270, to which a friend of the pastor was willing to add £100. The mortgage, and hence of course its interest, was reduced, and debts to the current treasurer, William Holtum, and to Alfred Kingsford were paid off. But by 1857 it was clear that they could not guarantee to pay Pitt's salary. There was no Home Mission then to come to the rescue. He was offered as much as the pew rents brought in, but he did not feel able to live on that, and in 1858 he resigned. The church was sorry to see him go. He preached a farewell sermon on 11th July and moved to a church in Burton-on-Trent. He left 145 members, 22 in the Bible class, and 148 in the Sunday School.

Again it was difficult to find a new pastor. This time the church was divided against itself. They considered a man called Ellison but the votes in favour of inviting him were only 24 against 17, with 9 abstentions. He was invited for a year, refused on those terms, was invited again but this time with a rider from the deacons that they could not advise his acceptance, and not unnaturally he then declined altogether. The rule was now established that a majority vote of two-thirds of the meeting was necessary to call a pastor, but the dissension and upheaval of those meetings could not have helped the work of the church. Nor did it help that they had no consistent teaching from the pulpit (twenty-eight different men had preached over the interregnum year), and a number of those not firmly committed to Salem – or perhaps to God – began to drift away.

At last they agreed to invite one of those whose preaching had been approved by several members, a man from a pastorate in Leicestershire named Alfred Ibberson. The decision was unanimous, and thankfully they took this to be the leading of God. In view of what was to follow it is difficult to know whether they were right.

Rev Alfred Ibberson

For the first few years of Ibberson's pastorate things seem to have gone fairly smoothly. More people were baptised and received into membership. Though money was still short there were no great financial crises. The number of members rose to its highest yet.

But while on the surface things were calm, after a while there began to be undercurrents of dissatisfaction among the church leaders. Ibberson was well-loved by the poorer people, but the better educated began to feel that both his teaching and his pastoral care left something to be desired. It is always difficult to put a finger on the exact signs of poor leadership, but it seems likely that Ibberson's ministry was high on emotional appeal and low on real wisdom and authority. On his part, of course, he may well have found that the church was not easy to lead. Some of the members were accustomed to running their own businesses and would not have taken easily to direction; some of them had been deacons for twenty-five years and probably had strong views on how God's work should be organised in this place. He increased the number of deacons from four to seven, but it does not seem to have helped.

All this culminated in January 1865 in a letter from the deacons to the pastor, setting out some of their concerns and asking for a meeting to discuss the matter. Ibberson's reaction was unfortunate. Instead of agreeing at least to meet and talk to the deacons, he seems to have flown onto the defensive immediately, rushed to gather support among the rest of the members and succeeded in dividing the church into two camps, those who were pro-minister against those who were pro-deacons. Battle ensued. Meetings were hastily convened, not always according to the rules. Alfred Kingsford wrote to 'The Freeman' newspaper, forerunner of the Baptist Times, ostensibly asking for advice but covering almost a column with criticisms of Ibberson, and this, as might be expected, roused even stronger feelings. Cries for the deacons' resignation were countered by cries for them to stay, but eventually a 61% majority favoured their resigning. They did so, and over the next few months they withdrew their membership from Salem altogether, leaving the church without their leadership – and incidentally without their financial support.

Perhaps the church felt some relief when they had gone, and hoped that it could now settle down to a more peaceful existence. But peace had been bought at a high price. Some of the most mature Christians of the church had left them, and over the next few years others also gradually withdrew. Many remained on the roll but ceased to take any part in the work and worship. Twice the roll was revised, and it was clear that the number in active membership was falling noticeably. Also, the proportion of men dwindled. By 1871 the roll stood at sixty-three names, and of these forty-six were women. No doubt many of these brought love and willing effort and Christian witness to the church, but most of them would have lacked education, experience of the world outside the home, and not least funds. Money was shorter than it had ever been, and not only was Alfred Kingsford no longer available to make loans in an emergency, but the mortgage on the chapel had to be increased to pay off a debt already owed him. They tried the experiment of putting boxes out on Sundays for freewill offerings; this had some small success, but the real money simply was not there. Widows' mites, however admirable in God's sight, do not by themselves pay a minister's stipend.

Ibberson struggled on. Till the end people were being baptised, including in 1869 four soldiers from the garrison in Dover. He was with the church for twelve years altogether, but he finally came to the point where he could cope no longer. His eyesight was failing. The church could not pay him even the £120 a year they had offered when he came, and the private income with which he had been supplementing his stipend till then had run out. He offered his resignation, and though the church passed a resolution hoping he would be able to stay, they had no actual means of fulfilling it. He resigned as minister in 1872, but remained a member.

In one of the large houses in Maison Dieu Road (opposite what is now the health centre) there lived at that time a young man who had been a captain in the Argyllshire Highlanders, Robert Townsend Passingham. He took services at Salem for several Sundays and was generally approved, and he was asked if he would take oversight of the church for five months. He was only twenty-eight, but he was a man accustomed to command. He also had private means, so he did not need the stipend they were unable to provide. He did not wish to be called Reverend, seeing, he said, no scriptural warrant for a division between laity and clergy, but the church called him Pastor, and he met with the deacons and began to assume the oversight at once.

Captain Robert Townsend Passingham

Unfortunately, this was not as straighforward as it sounded. Supported by the deacons he first proposed a number of minor changes: a new hymn-book, alterations to the notice-board, communion every Sunday and a weekly prayer-meeting. The church – that is, the very small number who still attended church meetings – agreed. But when some of the deacons suggested that the old quarrel be allowed to die, and that they should rescind the church's resolution that in 1865 had cut off Alfred Kingsford, his wife and five others from membership for a 'factious spirit', they met with instant opposition. Ibberson was still a member, and some of his flock still gave their allegiance to him. He demanded an amendment: this resolution could only be passed if Kingsford admitted that he had been in the wrong. The motion was carried by twelve votes to seven.

Passingham washed his hands of them. If they would not be guided, what was the point in his being there? He resigned immediately, and two of the deacons resigned with him. Just one, a supporter of Ibberson, was left to carry on as best he could. The church, which had just begun to feel that things were looking up, bowed its head under this new blow.

There is no record who in the end persuaded the two parties to be reconciled

Chapter 2

and allow the church to move forward again. It was Alfred Kingsford who in 1865 had written to 'The Freeman'. Now he was either persuaded, or decided himself under God's guidance, to send a second letter. He did not exactly apologise, but he admitted that it was sometimes easy to be mistaken, and said that he wished the matter might be laid to rest. Ibberson took this in the spirit that was intended, and responded with a near-apology of his own. Kingsford and the other six were re-admitted to the fellowship. Ibberson resigned his membership and moved away to live in Norfolk (though he kept contact with the church until he died in 1896). Passingham agreed to take over again, and the worst was over.

Captain Passingham was a man of strong views and vigorous energy. Now that he was genuinely in charge of the church he threw himself into the task of renewing its life and spirit. In five and a half years he saw many of the ex-members re-admitted and many new members received. By 1876 the roll had risen again to 122, and the church was once more a force for God.

A missionary society was formed, with a committee of ladies, the funds raised to be divided between the Baptist Missionary Society's home and foreign missions. A 'Dorcas society' was started, which would make clothes for the needy. The importance of prayer meetings was emphasised, and also the importance of all members attending church meetings. The church was actively considering doctrinal issues: when a speaker they felt to have unsound views on the subject of hell was proposed for the Baptist Union assembly meetings in 1874 they wrote protesting and threatening to withdraw from the Union if he was allowed to speak.

Not all Passingham's ideas worked. He would have liked all offerings to be voluntary, but eventually he agreed that this did not answer, and the subscription plan was renewed. But money was flowing again. When in 1874 they made a final effort and paid off the chapel debt they recorded their thanks to God for delivering them from 'this heavy and long-felt burden'. By the end of Passingham's ministry they were seeing a good balance each quarter and were able to pay him £40 and still see a small surplus – though on one occasion the surplus only amounted to two shillings and fourpence. But it seems unlikely that he had ever expected to stay permanently in the ministry.

In April 1876 he suggested that an assistant minister might be appointed to help him. In July of the same year he offered a better plan. There was a minister in Redruth, Cornwall, who would be excellent for this pastorate. They would be hearing him, the Rev. E. J. Edwards, preach on two Sundays, the 11th and 18th of February 1877. As they listened, would they consider inviting him to be their minister? He duly preached on the 11th and 18th, and on Monday 19th they held a special church meeting. From the meeting they sent three elders to where Edwards was staying with an invitation to the pastorate, and the three came back before the end of the meeting bringing his acceptance.

Rev Elijah John Edwards

He could not leave Cornwall immediately, and Passingham remained until he was free; at the last church meeting where Passingham presided the church noted their great gratitude to him for his untiring efforts for the church and the work of God. He remained a church member for some years and the church kept contact with him until his death in 1893.

So in July 1877 Elijah Edwards began his ministry at Salem. He was an able man. He had won a prize for mathematics at school and as a young man he worked as an accountant in the City of London; he read Latin and spoke fluent French and Italian. He was the eldest of four brothers, all of whom became either ministers or missionaries. He was trained at the college that was then called simply the Pastors' College (founded by C. H. Spurgeon and later to become Spurgeon's College) and training and intelligence together seem to have made him an excellent organiser, besides being a man of vision. It was Salem's good fortune that such a man was willing to spend most of his working life obeying God's call to the leadership of a comparatively unimportant church in a comparatively small town. He was to minister at Salem for twenty-five years.

He was not a man of dramatic action, and his ministry began quietly. But numbers, which had been increasing under Passingham, continued to increase, and the building which in 1840 had seemed adequate began to strain at the

Chapter 2

seams. The Sunday school, particularly, now numbering two hundred and fifty, needed more room, and the idea of making galleries in the chapel itself, which had been considered once or twice before, began to seem very necessary. All this would, of course, need considerable funding, and though money was not as short as it had been, they were still not rich. Could they raise enough?

In 1879 the South Eastern Railway and the London, Chatham and Dover Railway were working together to extend the railway line from Dover to join up with the line at Deal, and a contractor called T.A. Walker, who was working on the new line, came to live in Dover. He brought his wife, four daughters and three nephews, and the family came to Salem to worship, but they were a little put out to find that there was not room for them to sit all together in one pew. Mr Walker was a man of action, and he felt that something should be done. He brought to the pastor a suggested plan for a new schoolroom and galleries; these would cost an estimated £1000 to build, but he offered to carry out the work himself for £700, considering the extra cost his contribution to the work of God in Dover. Pastor and church felt that this was definitely God's leading, and they began to discuss ways to raise the money.

It took a year to carry out all the plans, and the final cost borne by Mr Walker was considerably higher than the £1000 estimate. But in May 1880 the chapel was re-opened. There was room at last for all the adults and all the children, with seats to spare in case the church continued to grow. In fact there was room for the Kent & Sussex Baptist Association to hold their annual meetings at Salem in June of that year. The church patted itself on the back, and perhaps it hoped to sit back and rest for a while.

But the church is not buildings, but people. No doubt working together with a specific object in view had helped to weld them into a stronger whole. But their pastor did not consider that now they had nothing more to aim for. In the association letter of 1885 he said without much enthusiasm, 'The work in the town has been of the ordinary kind, with some measure of blessing'. Now that they had the buildings finished they should be getting on with the real business of the church, the saving of souls

In 1886 a man called Henry Varley came to Dover to lead a series of meetings. They had a great impact in the town, and at Salem over the following fifteen months sixty-eight people were baptised. The church was delighted, not because the numbers in the pews were increasing (though no doubt they found that an encouragement as well) but because people's lives were being changed.

Other events took place, of course, over these early years of Edwards' ministry. In 1886 there were special collections and a tea held for some of the town's unemployed. An organ no longer used by Sittingbourne parish church was bought and fitted in Salem – with some difficulty and expense. The mission stations at Ewell Minnis, Temple Ewell and St Margaret's were brought more closely under Salem's aegis at this time, and during the last quarter of the century all three acquired buildings for regular use. The roof at Salem was repaired.

But one of the pastor's strengths was that he never lost the vision of his church as an evangelising force. In 1887 he was urging his people to increased diligence in seeking the salvation of souls. In 1889 and 1890 more meetings were held, though they did not have the impact of the 1886 meetings. Then in 1892 a united mission was held in the town by Messrs. Fullerton and Smith, and 'many souls were blessed'. And these were only the special events. Edwards was a sound, if not flamboyant, preacher, and throughout this time the numbers at Salem were growing steadily. By the end of the century they had passed three hundred.

Nor did they confine their efforts to this country. In 1889 Elijah Edwards' brother, Ebenezer Edwards, who was a missionary in China, visited and spoke to the church. This fired enthusiasm among the members. Over the years they collected money for various individual causes as well as for the Baptist Missionary Society, and several members accepted the call themselves to go

---

. . . We were made to mourn in common with so many Christians the bereavement of the Church Universal by the death of our beloved friend Mr C.H. Spurgeon   *(Association letter 1892)*

Chapter 2

out to the mission field. George and Margaret Stokes were working in China during the Boxer Rebellion and were among those who were killed there.

As the new century dawned the church was strong and stable. Elijah Edwards had been pastor for twenty-three years and was loved and honoured not only by his own people but by many in the town. But a church of more than three hundred souls is large for one man to oversee. Edwards was a conscientious shepherd to his flock. His letter of acceptance to the pastorate is one of the few early ones that does not mention the question of annual holidays. He never missed chairing a church meeting, and his regular visiting of his people was much appreciated. He was involved in local evangelism, and was president of the newly formed Dover Free Church Council. But he was not growing any younger, and by the turn of the century the work seems to have become too much for him. At the end of 1901 his health broke down.

The church was thrown back on its own resources for the first time most of its people could remember. They considered anxiously what they could do to help the pastor. They insisted that he take two months leave of absence, and when he was not fully better by then and asked apologetically for longer, offering to pay for preachers to supply the pulpit for another three weeks, they agreed to the leave but categorically refused the payment. But something more was needed. They considered their finances and decided that with a little extra effort they could afford to pay £120 a year to a young man from college to be Assistant Pastor and take some of the burden from Elijah Edwards.

The man they invited was Frederick John Skinner. He was twenty-nine, an attractive personality and a persuasive preacher. He had entered Spurgeon's College with his heart set on becoming a missionary, but at the end of his studies it had been decided that he was not strong enough to cope with the rigours of the mission field and so he was available to Salem when they called. He was recognised at the beginning of June 1902, and the church – and probably Edwards too - breathed a sigh of relief. With help the pastor could surely go on for several more years, training up the new man and gradually letting go of the reins himself. It seemed an ideal situation.

However, man proposes but God disposes. Perhaps they should have been warned by the doctors' refusal to let Skinner go abroad. For seven weeks he carried out his new duties at Salem. Edwards was still far from well, and Skinner preached mornings and evenings on Sundays and began other pastoral work. He attracted young people, and was well liked. On Sunday 27th July, it is recorded in his obituary, 'he preached in the evening a most remarkable sermon, and a hush fell on the people as they heard his impassioned appeal to the unconverted'. But perhaps he was already unwell, for at the end of the service he felt very weary. The next day he was prostrate with 'enteric fever' – probably typhoid, which was still endemic in England at that time. A strong man might have survived it, but Skinner was not strong, and on the Tuesday, 'to the intense grief and surprise of all', he died.

Rev Frederick John Skinner

The memorial plaque recording this so brief ministry is still to be seen on the wall at Salem. The church, which had written so eagerly to the Association in May 1902 about Skinner's appointment 'we are looking forward to a period of increased useful service in this town and district', had to write the following year recording his death.

Without an assistant Elijah Edwards did not feel that he could carry on, and in October 1902 he tendered his resignation. Loth to accept it, the church asked if he would consider becoming Assistant Pastor, with no duties at all but with £60 of the stipend that would have gone to Skinner. He agreed, and this situation remained until his death in 1908. But now they must start looking not for an assistant but for a new pastor.

1902–3 was an unsettled year. There were one or two other resignations about this time of long-standing church officers. There were difficulties in carrying on some of the church's activities. Even the money they had hoped to present to Edwards as a memorial gift was slow in coming in. Clearly the loss of their leader had thrown the whole church off balance. But in 1903 things looked up. Walter Holyoak, then minister at Tenterden, was invited

Chapter 2

to the pastorate by a 'practically unanimous' vote, and accepted. He was to remain twenty-eight years, longer than Elijah Edwards himself.

The church that he took over at the turn of the century was similar in many ways to the church of 1839. The make-up of the town had changed somewhat; the large pool of domestic servants was fast disappearing, and there were far fewer self-employed small craftsmen working from a room behind the shop. White-collar jobs had replaced blue-collar for a proportion of the membership. But the members were still drawn mainly from the lower middle class and respectable working class. The difference now was that this was a second generation of Salem people. Many of them had grown up in Salem. Sons followed their fathers into membership and often into leadership. There was a tremendous loyalty among them, with deacons serving for twenty-five years or more. And over the years customs that had grown up had become hallowed traditions.

The danger was that the organisation would take over. It would have been so easy to ride along on the habits of the past, letting things go on as they had for twenty, thirty, forty years, continuing the missionary collections, the Sunday School classes, even the evangelistic meetings, just because that was what Salem had always done.

But in fact the church seems to have avoided this. Although the minutes become increasingly formal and detailed at this time, they still reflect a genuine enthusiasm and commitment to God's cause. Numbers did not rise any further, but at a time when a speaker was commenting sadly at one of the BU Assemblies on the contrast between the number of new buildings going up and the way overall membership was going down, Salem held its own. By 1932, at the end of the ministry, there were still more than three hundred members. And they did not merely keep the old activities alive, they began new ones, always striving to reach out to the people beyond their walls.

The pattern of Walter Holyoak's ministry shows interesting parallels with Elijah Edwards'. He began by reorganising things a little, conducting a thorough revision of the church roll, introducing a new hymn-book (an activity new ministers are prone to) and appointing District Visitors. Then in 1904 it was decided that the Sunday School, then about four hundred and

Rev and Mrs Walter Holyoak

fifty strong, was finding even the rooms in the 1880 building too small. An extra piece of ground behind the chapel was bought and they began to raise money for an extension.

They needed about £3000 – an immense sum for those days – and it was five years before they could even begin to build. But in September of 1909, with over £1700 still to be found, the first stone was laid, and in June 1910 the buildings were opened, a hall, classrooms, and a lobby linking the new building with the old. The earliest memories of some of the present Salem members are of Sunday School meetings in those rooms off Edwards Road.

In the meantime the ordinary work of the church went on. They appreciated the efforts of their new pastor, and in January 1905 they voted him an increase on his stipend, noting the 'very able manner in which he had directed and controlled the church'. Work at Ewell Minnis had been under Salem's care some thirty years earlier but had closed; now a group of Salem's young people started it up again, and in 1912 the Wesleyan Methodists, who owned it, handed over the hall to Salem. In 1908 a Boys Life Brigade company was formed at Salem. A mission was held and twenty-seven people were converted.

Naturally, not everything was perfect. The singing at some of the services could be half-hearted and there were protests about the unfamiliar tunes in the new hymn-book. Church meetings did not always run smoothly. The attendance at the week-night prayer meetings could be scanty and over the years they tried several different days and times to see if it made a difference. But in general the work was alive and purposeful.

More missions were held. A Girls Life Brigade company was started. Several young men of the church applied to become missionaries. Days of prayer were held regularly each year. And so they came in June 1914 to the church's

Chapter 2

75th anniversary. They held a week of celebrations, including Sunday services conducted by Elijah Edwards' brother, T. Llewellyn Edwards, an evangelistic meeting for young people, services at the mission chapels, and a lecture on 'Baptists in Dover' by Walter Holyoak, the text of which was also printed as a booklet, a comprehensive survey of the various Baptist causes in Dover from very early days. No doubt as they celebrated they looked back and thanked God for his goodness to the church so far, but when they looked forward they must have wondered what lay ahead. Six weeks later war was to break out.

Almost immediately it brought changes to Salem. Dover was a garrison town, and even while the front line was way across Europe there were ships sailing from the harbour and troops moving through its streets. The fledgling Girls Life Brigade was closed down. A proposed mission by the united free churches was cancelled, and a plan for Salem to take over the chapel at East Langdon from the Primitive Methodists was left in abeyance for the time being – never in fact to be resurrected. The church premises were insured against damage by aircraft and bombardment, the senior members and officers of the Boys Life Brigade offered their services for ambulance work among the wounded expected in Dover, and a War Sufferers Helpers Association was formed to assist refugees. Soon there were casualties among the members and congregation. A number of men were killed in action, but perhaps one of the saddest deaths was that of a boy, Francis Hall, who was killed on his way to Sunday School at Salem in 1916 by a bomb dropped from a German seaplane.

However, the ordinary work of the church – as of the town – went on. Sunday services and week-night meetings continued as usual. On Sunday afternoon teas were organised for the troops in the neighbourhood, and many of the men stayed on to swell the numbers at the evening service. In 1915, despite the war, the Kent and Sussex Baptist Association held its annual meetings as usual, and this year held them at Salem.

There was, though, 'general distraction and preoccupation due to the War'. Numbers at church meetings fell exceptionally low, and in 1916 it was impossible to find delegates to attend the Baptist Union Assembly in London.

By this time twenty-two of the church members were serving in the forces, and others were engaged in transport service, munitions, and ambulance and nursing work. The soldiers' teas on Sundays continued, and by 1917 they had become so popular that there were too many men for the hall and for the available money, and a limit had to be put on numbers. By now conditions generally were deteriorating. What with the blackout and the risk of air-raids the church decided that it must alter the times of evening services and meetings to the late afternoon, and that the New Year Social and Watch Night Service should be cancelled altogether. On the Sunday School anniversary they decided to cancel the evening service, and they were thankful they had when that night's air-raid took place earlier than usual, at just the time when they would have been meeting.

But the war did not last for ever. On Wednesday November 13th 1918 and on the Sunday following they held thanksgiving services for the signing of the Armistice. A memorial plaque was put up to those connected with Salem who had died. Food controls had been instituted nationally, and the Food Control Committee took over Salem school hall for a while. And the church began to get back to normal.

Walter Holyoak and his wife were hard-working people and totally dedicated to the life of the church. Twice more during the next twenty years the Pastor's stipend was raised, and in 1921 the church made a special effort and raised the money for them to go on a once-in-a-lifetime holiday to Switzerland. They were obviously well loved and respected. In 1915 the Baptist Union had introduced a scheme called the 'Ministerial Settlement and Sustentation' plan, which encouraged churches, among other things, to re-consider the pastor's appointment at intervals of five years. In 1925 there was a quarterly church meeting attended by a hundred and forty-nine members – an unheard-of number, the usual attendance being between twenty and fifty – and the Pastor was invited to remain by a unanimous vote. Forty-two letters were also received in agreement from those who could not get to the meeting. In 1930 the attendance was a hundred and sixteen, with twenty-seven letters in support, and the result was the same.

However, by this time the Pastor was getting older. In 1931 he was ill and

Chapter 2

unable to take services for ten consecutive Sundays, and he began to feel, as Elijah Edwards had done before him, that the work at Salem was too much. If he stayed, he said, he might go on for another four or five years and then have to give up the ministry altogether, whereas he might be able to carry on for longer if he moved to another church where his duties were lighter. More than a hundred people gathered at a church meeting in September 1931 to receive, with great regret, his resignation. They recorded their love and respect, their deep gratitude, and their prayer that the lightened load at Tenterden would result in the complete restoration of his health. (In fact he never seems to have recovered fully. He retired from the ministry at Tenterden in 1936 because of ill-health, and lived for eight more years in increasing weakness until he died in 1944 at the age of seventy-three.)

Between them Elijah Edwards and Walter Holyoak had led the church for fifty-four years; they were years which might be considered Salem's golden age. Over three hundred members had worked together, worshipped together, had been taught thoroughly and authoritatively the Christian doctrines, and had reached out to the people in Dover and the villages. During these years the work at Ewell Minnis had been re-started, and a chapel built at St Margaret's. An extension had been built at Temple Ewell for the Sunday School, and work had recently been started and a chapel built at Capel-le-Ferne. In 1932 there were 36 Sunday School teachers at Salem, 20 local preachers serving the villages, and 11 missionaries closely associated with the church. There was a GLB, Christian Endeavour, boys' and girls' Bible Classes, a Women's Social Meeting and a Young People's Fellowship with a Play Centre for the children. There were weekly prayer meetings and regular weeks for special prayer. When Holyoak left it was the end of an era.

The man who took over from him in 1932 was another Spurgeon's student, Stanley Tweed. The church had heard three other prospective ministers, but the 'pulpit committee' could not reach agreement on any of them. However, the committee was unanimous in bringing Stanley Tweed's name to the church and a very large majority agreed to call him.

He was 36 when he came to Dover in 1932. Walter Holyoak, of course, had also been a young man when he began his ministry. But that was twenty-nine years ago, and by now the church was used to a father figure, a man who had taught many of them from their earliest days, a man with strong, even severe opinions, a man of presence and authority. Now the world, and the church, was changing. Stanley Tweed was of a new generation, with new ideas. For most of his ministry he seems to have been trying desperately to steer a steady course between those who clung firmly to the old ways and the old values and those who rejoiced at the opportunity to try something new.

The first problem was of finding a Manse. Until now Salem ministers had lived in rented accommodation. But it was becoming more usual for people to buy their own homes, and it was difficult to find a suitable house to rent for the minister. Eventually they bought a house at 285 Folkestone Road, which cost them £900. Finances were not too healthy, and the efforts to pay off this sum hampered them until the end of the ministry.

However, the new minister moved in, and the ministry began happily, in a continuation of the warmth and unity which had been particularly noticeable in Holyoak's last years. Numbers continued steady on Sundays and also at the Thursday evening meetings, to the gratification of the new Pastor, who hoped they might even increase. The Sunday School held a second 'decision Sunday' (the first had been in 1931) and forty children responded, some of whom were baptised on Christmas Day 1932 and became life-long members of Salem.

But before long small disputes began to ruffle the waters. The Bible Class wanted to perform sketches in the church: was someone checking that the sketches were suitable? Why was the choir allowed to hold its social during what was supposed to be reserved as a week of prayer? Should the women's sewing clubs be allowed to make and sell things for the benefit of the Manse fund? Could the young people form a Social Club, and if so, what rules were to be laid down? Should they be allowed (what is the world coming to!) to play billiards? A good deal of time was spent at church meetings dealing with this kind of question, and the feeling comes through that the Pastor was not altogether as strong as he might have been in directing his flock.

More significant, perhaps, were the problems that began to arise in spiritual matters. There was some unease about the work of the Sunday School, and several members were asked to become teachers but refused. In 1937 new Superintendents were needed for Capel and Temple Ewell but none could be found. The Christian Endeavour society closed down and a social club took its place. In 1938 the church was discussing how it was going to celebrate its hundredth anniversary the following year, and among the suggestions – special services, a reunion gathering, an extra fund-raising effort – a plea was raised that surely there should be some kind of evangelistic outreach. It was passed by and fell instantly into oblivion. The ship was not sinking, but there were clearly cracks close to the water-line.

How this ministry would have ended if times had been normal it is impossible to say. But in 1939, before the centenary events could take place, war broke out. The carefully planned celebrations were cancelled. Once again Dover became a place of disruption and danger. And in 1941 Stanley Tweed heard the call of God to go and serve as a chaplain in the RAF, and Salem was without a minister once more.

It was not an easy time for a church to be pastorless. Dover was a front-line town, with the enemy, for a good part of the war, just twenty-two miles away across the Channel. It suffered repeated air-raids, and uniquely it suffered shelling from the guns on the French coast that were aimed at the military bases and shipping in the Channel but frequently hit the town instead. Members' homes and the church premises alike suffered damage from bombs and shells. Children and old people were evacuated and there were plans in the event of an invasion to evacuate the rest of the civilian population; in fact the pastor and the caretaker were paid in advance for three months in 1940 in anticipation of such an event.

Air-raids and blackout meant the change of service times. Many Salem members were conscripted or moved away to safer areas. By 1941 only two deacons were left in Dover to carry the leadership. Two had moved away and did not expect to come back, the others would be back sometime but did not know when. They offered to resign and let others be appointed if that would help, though the church did not take them up on this but co-opted a few non-deacons instead to help with the leadership for the duration of the war. Congregations were small, and most of Salem's activities, especially in

> **'** Mr Stefforn asked if Pastor could be supplied with new baptismal garments, as he had noticed how leaky the others had become.**'**
>
> (Church Minutes April 1945)

the winter months, had to be curtailed or cancelled.

Still, they carried on as best they could. The Sunday School managed to continue meeting throughout the war with those children who were not evacuated or who had eventually filtered back, even the tiny ones meeting for part of the time in a house in de Burgh Street. Quite early in the war the church had once again opened a canteen in the lecture hall where servicemen off duty could relax, write letters and buy cheap refreshments – and cigarettes – and this was where those left in Dover concentrated much of their effort. A good number of the soldiers responded by coming to the services on Sundays. The primary building had been taken over once again by the Food and Coal Control offices, who at least paid rent for it, which was very thankfully received while congregations were small and offerings low.

They were without a minister for more than a year, and it is a tribute to the members that they carried on as well as they did in such difficult conditions. When they wrote to a prospective minister, Leonard Bayly, in 1942, they felt it necessary to stress 'the present war conditions existing in Dover and the possibility that life may get more exacting and difficult'. There was very little money to pay a minister, and there was a suggestion that he might give oversight to Deal and Walmer who were also without ministers at the time and they might contribute to his salary, but this plan eventually fell through. The Baptist Union gave £20 from its Sustentation Fund and promised £85 per year from its Emergency Fund at least for the duration of the war. The rest of the £300 they offered Salem had to find for themselves.

In fact, money seems to have become less of a problem from now on. A house in Shakespeare Road had been given to the church in 1939 and sold, and this had helped to pay off the Manse debt. The other funds increased steadily over the next few years and the worrying deficits each quarter

Chapter 2

disappeared. The rent from the Fuel Office helped, of course. War damage was covered by the Government's compensation scheme, and there was enough left in the Canteen Fund at the end of the war to allow for the renovation and re-decoration of the rooms that had been used. Despite the post-war austerity (or perhaps because of it, there being nothing else to spend money on) money was no longer as short as it had been.

Leonard Bayly took up his ministry in 1943. He was another Spurgeon's student. He had had a pastorate in Sheerness for four years before he came to Salem, but perhaps he was still inexperienced. He was a quieter man than Tweed, rather pedantic, happier in dealing with individuals than groups and given to doing good by stealth. The young people called him Bill Bailey and enjoyed his company (two young ladies of his congregation fought for the privilege of ironing his shirts when his wife had a baby) but there seem to have been reservations among some of the older members. It can't have been an easy period to take leadership, first the 'exacting and difficult' war years, and then the years after the war when the members who had left gradually trickled back, no doubt expecting to find Salem as they had left it and discovering how much things had changed while they were away.

Slowly it became more and more obvious that there was an absence of that unity and purpose that the church had felt in Holyoak's time. Both pastor and deacons felt it, but it was not easy to decide what to do about it. Numbers had been falling slowly but inexorably since Holyoak had left. Of course Salem was not alone in this – church-going was declining everywhere – but in 1946 the diaconate was pointing out to the church meeting that 'the membership and effectiveness of the church had declined; since 1932 we had suffered a nett loss of one third of our membership; the average age of members was increasing which meant that the situation would become increasingly serious. At the present rate, in ten years the membership would be only a quarter what it was twenty years ago.' At the new year they sent out a letter asking all the members to re-covenant themselves, but it had no lasting effect. Somehow the minister seems not to have been able to inspire them to reach out to the war-weary people around them and draw them in.

In May 1946 the suggestion was raised that perhaps what Salem needed was an assistant minister. The branch chapels were still in difficulties and the idea was that an assistant minister would have special responsibility for them, not to replace the Superintendents and local preachers but to help and encourage them. He would also be able to give the minister a hand with routine administration at Salem. It is true that in the past St Margaret's and Temple Ewell had been cared for by full-time workers, and now there was Capel to be overseen as well as the others. On the other hand, the church roll was only two-thirds of the size that Edwards and Holyoak had dealt with single-handed. Perhaps an assistant minister would have helped, but it is doubtful whether it was the whole solution. In fact, though the chapels were in favour of the idea and pledged themselves to help support the extra man, the idea died a natural death because in 1947 a more fundamental issue arose.

When Stanley Tweed had been appointed in 1932 he had objected to the five year limit to the pastorate, and the church had waived it. However, when they called Leonard Bayly they returned to the old plan, so he had

Dover (Salem) Baptist Church

BALLOT PAPER - Mar. 20th, 1947

Are you in favour of the Pastor's engagement being extended beyond December next ?

YES	
NO	

Voting slip on the extension of Leonard Bayly's ministry

been invited for a period of five years, which would now need to be extended by the vote of the church meeting. Eighty-four people came to the special church meeting in March of 1947 for that purpose – and a difficult meeting it was.

The matter was confused by the fact that the pastor said he would much prefer the time limit to be eliminated altogether, so that he could be elected for an indefinite period. This is understandable: a pastor needs to be able to take a long view and form long-term plans, and if he knows he may be dismissed in a short while he may all too easily find himself, like the Government, constantly looking over his shoulder and trying to placate the electorate. The church was divided on the point, uncertain whether to insist or to let it go. A long time was spent talking round the subject, and it did not help that they could not decide whether to deal with this point first or whether to take the vote for re-election first and then go back to it. The chairing of the meeting seems to have left something to be desired. At last they agreed to vote first on the re-election. A 60% majority was needed for him to stay. The vote was taken, and he gained only 57%. So the question of the time-limit became irrelevant: his ministry at Salem was suddenly over.

Perhaps it was true, as some people said, that members were confused by this time about what exactly they were voting for, though the wording on the voting papers seems clear enough. At any rate, Leonard Bayly did not take the decision easily. In a statement to the church after he had left, the deacons complained vigorously of his conduct. He had made it difficult for the deacons to work with him, they said. He had come to the re-election meeting against their advice, he had criticised their leading of the meeting and claimed that the vote did not reflect the real wishes of the members. He had used the pulpit to state his case, and had even urged his own views about their next appointment at his farewell meeting. The protests have an oddly familiar ring: they take one back to the animadversions of Alfred Kingsford almost a century earlier on the conduct of Alfred Ibberson. In both cases there was probably right and wrong on both sides.

But whatever the truth of the matter, Leonard Bayly had finished his time at Salem. He left at the end of 1947 and went on to a pastorate in Brixton. He continued in the ministry for the next thirty years, and there is no suggestion that his other churches were unhappy with him.

It is interesting to note that in Salem's history a unanimous call to a minister does not necessarily mean a successful pastorate, and a divided call does not necessarily mean an unsuccessful one. Alfred Ibberson had a unanimous vote, Leonard Bayly very nearly so, and in both cases the pastorate ended in dissension. Now, in 1948, the church had some difficulty in reaching a decision. Fifteen men were considered by the 'vacancy committee', several came to preach, one man was almost called but did not quite get the 80% of the votes that they had decided was needed. The vote that finally led to the new minister's call was 81.7 %, only just over the borderline – and yet he proved to be a most capable pastor and stayed eleven years.

Islwyn Eurog Evans was trained at South Wales Baptist College, and had been in ministry at Willesden in north west London for five years before he came to Dover. He was 34 when he came, a little, energetic Welshman with the 'gift of the gab' in his speaking. The fact that many of his congregation referred to him as 'Taff' may be understandable in view of his two unpronounceable Christian names, but it also says how easy the relationship was. Like his immediate predecessors, he was good with the young people. He came along to the Youth Club's meetings, got to know them and played table tennis with them, and very soon at Sunday evening services the galleries were full of young people. He was an excellent preacher; in fact there was a suggestion in 1949, though the plan was not in the end found practicable, that his sermons should be printed. He preached apparently without notes and held everyone's attention for as long as he spoke. (That is, most of the time – and if there were occasionally those among his young listeners who were more interested in the opposite sex in the other gallery than in the sermon, the minister was not slow to notice it and did not hesitate to mention it to them after the service).

People had been joining the church by baptism throughout the previous ministries, but the numbers increased now. Seven people were baptised in the same month that Islwyn Evans arrived, seven in the following year, fourteen in 1950 and nineteen in 1954. This did not increase the total

Chapter 2

membership because there were deaths and transfers and erasures on the debit side, but the numbers that had been falling steadied again. All the church's activities seem to have been revitalised. The Girls Life Brigade was restarted and later the Boys Brigade, and a new Young People's Fellowship begun. In 1952 reports were given to the church from the Men's Fellowship, Women's Meeting, Sunday School, Choir, Missionary Council, Youth Fellowship, Bible Class, GLB and Young Wives and Mothers' Meeting. Young people were encouraged not only to gather and enjoy themselves at their own meetings but to give service in the Sunday School and other organisations. And between 1952 and 1960 no fewer than five young men from Salem were recommended for training for the Baptist ministry. (One of these fell by the wayside, but Ernie Clipsham, John Hopper, John A. Hopper and Roy Connor went on to long and useful service in the ministry.)

The church looked beyond its own walls, too. There was an 'inner mission' in 1950 (for the church only), which led to a 'crusade' in 1951 (for those outside the church). There seemed to be little visible result from this at the time, but perhaps seeds had been planted. In 1955 the free churches of Dover combined to put on the Billy Graham film 'Souls in Conflict' at the Plaza cinema, and one hundred and eight people responded then and there to its message. How many of those had first been made aware of God's calling at Salem's earlier crusade?

There were, as always, financial worries. In 1956 the Fuel Office finally stopped hiring the hall, which meant a loss of their three pounds per week rent. A meeting was held the following year to discuss the situation. Average expenses were now £23 per week, the church was told, and income only £17. What were they to do? Various suggestions were made and referred back to the deacons, and some of them were eventually implemented. There were some who said that what was needed was more prayer - that if the spiritual position was improved, the financial situation would follow - and the pastor supported them. Whether they prayed or not we do not know. Certainly there was some effect from the meeting, for income increased, but it did not increase as much as they hoped, and pleas for more people to support the Envelope Scheme, putting a regular contribution by in an envelope each Sunday, were heard for some years to come.

Another problem rose out of the very success of the pastor with the young people. Many were responding to his message, accepting salvation and being baptised. But perhaps not all of them realised fully what this would involve because after a time some were drifting away, and the church came with some surprise to realise that the solid, regular Bible Study that had been an accepted thing in Walter Holyoak's time was still necessary to nurture the spiritual babies.

But in general this has to be considered a successful ministry. Islwyn Evans had been called, of course, for five years, and in 1953 the church met to consider whether to extend the invitation. This time they got things right. The minister was not present at the voting – though he was obviously waiting somewhere else in the building to be called in afterwards. First they voted on whether to extend the call. The result was a unanimous Yes, and it was announced 'amid applause'. Then they took a second vote on whether to cancel the five-year time limit, and again the votes were overwhelmingly in favour. They then invited the Pastor to come and hear the result. Someone had discovered since 1947 how to chair a meeting.

Responding to the re-invitation the Pastor said that the past four and a half years had not been easy, and he commented on the necessity of work to build a fellowship, but he said that he had never before experienced such working of the Church together. He charged them to join together more and more deeply in prayer and to cultivate the spiritual view of the Church. These two emphases, on work and prayer – together with his gift for uniting and inspiring the people – no doubt account to a large extent for the ministry's success.

It is sad, in a way, that a man who could lead a church so ably did not go on when he left to lead other congregations elsewhere, but he felt that this was not where he was called. He stayed at Salem for eleven years, and there are present members who remember him with affection. Perhaps he sensed that though he had done his best to unite the older and younger members of his congregation, his real flair was for working with the young. When he resigned in 1959 it was to leave the ministry and take an appointment in charge of religious education at Glyn Grammar School, Epsom. He joined the Castle Street church there, though, and his gift for preaching was highly regarded in that area for the six years until his illness and early death in 1966.

When he left Dover the Moderator told a rather stunned church that the vacancy of the pastorate was a challenge to them. A 'vacancy committee' was set up and seems to have worked briskly at its task. In April 1960 a new minister was appointed and he was inducted on July 23rd of the same year.

Berkeley John Johnson was born in London, and had held pastorates in London, Nottinghamshire and Sussex before he came to Dover. He was a quiet, scholarly man. He was born in the same year as Islwyn Evans, which meant that one was 45 when he left Salem and the other was 45 when he arrived, making him one of the oldest of the men beginning ministry here.

In many ways Berkeley Johnson followed in the footsteps of his two great predecessors, Elijah Edwards and Walter Holyoak. He worked very hard and rarely looked to his own interests. He chaired the meetings of all the

Rev Berkeley John Johnson with Roger and Jonathan Wheeler

organisations, faithfully visited the sick and house-bound, gave hospitality to the lonely, typed and ran off the monthly newsletter, and sometimes took three services on a Sunday, two at Salem and a third at one of the chapels. He was Moderator of the KSBA in 1965–6, president of the Dover Free Church Council in 1967–8, and Secretary to the Baptist Building Fund from 1973 to 1992. In short he gave himself without stint to the work of God. If hard work and care for his flock make a good pastor then Berkeley Johnson was an excellent one.

He took over a church full of life and activity. There was a strong core of people faithful and dedicated to God's work, many of them young people abounding with energy and enthusiasm. The services were well attended. They held socials and coffee mornings and garden parties, sang carols on the chapel steps at Christmas, and walked to the beach between the New Year social and the Watch-night service and to Eythorne for the older church's Good Friday anniversary.

But changes came with the new ministry. Berkeley Johnson was a very different man from Islwyn Evans. His services were formal, rather restrained, his Bible studies a scaled-down version of Sunday worship. The congregation would always call him 'Mr Johnson' – seldom 'Berkeley', and never in a million years by a nickname. He was friendly with individuals, but kept the business of the church firmly in the hands of himself and the deacons, very much as Edwards and Holyoak had done before him. It was a style of leadership which needed absolute faith in the minister's ability and inspiration, and whereas in the nineteen twenties many of the people had left school at twelve or thirteen and were happy to trust to his superior understanding, in the sixties most of them had had five years or more of secondary education, and the one-man government was not universally appreciated. Over the next few years membership slid imperceptibly down again.

Partly, too, this was because Berkeley Johnson had not Evans' gift of reaching the younger members. The youth organisations, deprived of enthusiasm from the top, began to wilt a little. The Sunday School continued, and the Girls Brigade flourished, chiefly because of the dedicated captaincy of Doris Cook and then Iris Skegg. But the Boys Brigade, restarted in 1957, closed again and the youth club numbers rose and fell, depending very much on the availability and the quality of its leaders. Those young people who were baptised in the sixties were chiefly the children of church members.

However, Salem was still a stable church, and the members were happy enough with their pastor to re-invite him after five years and then to abolish the time limit altogether. And around nineteen sixty something else began to happen, which was to draw the people closer together and begin a new chapter in the church's history. The chapel that had been built near the edge of the expanding town in 1840 was now right in the centre of the shopping area and taking up a site ideal for commercial purposes. Around this time no fewer than eight businesses, in Dover and elsewhere, wrote to the church asking if they were interested in selling their land. By now parts of the building were a hundred and twenty years old and seemed constantly in need of repair. It was large and cumbersome and difficult to heat, and there was nowhere for the congregation to park their cars on Sundays. Were these letters the voice of God telling them to move to up-to-date premises elsewhere?

It was a hard decision, perhaps easier for the minister who had come recently to Salem than for those who had been brought up in this building and whose parents and grandparents had worshipped there. In 1961 when further enquiries had been made and the move seemed a definite possibility a church meeting was held. The hundred and twenty-year-old trust deed of the chapel allowed only male members to vote, but the ladies were encouraged to come and put their point of view, and it seems that on the whole the distaff side would have preferred to stay in Biggin Street. But eventually the vote was carried by thirteen (male) votes to five that they should leave.

In fact it was more than ten years before they actually moved into the new building. Finding a suitable new site, agreeing a buyer for the old site, making application to the charity commissioners for permission to sell - it all took time. But at last, in 1968, the Biggin Street site was sold and a site bought in Maison Dieu Road. There would be room for a church and halls, all on one level, with a small garden and a good-sized car-park, and the difference between the price of the old site and the new would, they hoped, be enough to pay for the erection of the new building. Boots the Chemists Ltd wanted to take over the old site as soon as possible so the church moved into a prefabricated building on its new site and watched the new sanctuary being raised next door. In April 1973 they held the dedication service in the new Salem Baptist Church.

The rest of Berkeley Johnson's ministry ran smoothly. Perhaps the church was a little inward-looking; murmurs of visits to the neighbourhood faded away again without perceptible outcome. Church meetings could sometimes be stormy. But there were baptisms, and the numbers on roll stayed fairly steady for the rest of the decade. Though the Salem prayer-meeting was never very well attended prayer groups began to meet in one or two homes. In 1975 a special event was arranged, 'Salem 75', with a weekend of special services, a musical evening, exhibitions of old documents and photos and people's handicrafts, flower arrangements, and articles for sale. Sales of Work were frowned upon as giving the wrong message – and also as giving a poor return for all the work involved - but this had the same advantages, encouraging the church and congregation to work together to a common end, and it was generally enjoyed. A small profit was in fact made, which went to buying comfortable chairs for the crèche.

In those days of spiralling inflation the minister's stipend was raised yearly between 1971 and 1975, and eventually pegged so that it never fell below the BU minimum (though it never rose above it either). Finances in general were more or less stable, though there were the usual fairly regular pleas for more giving to the Church, to the Home Work Fund, and to pay off debts on the new building. The building itself had teething troubles – problems with the heating system in fact ran on for many years – but in general the church was happy in its new place. It was the calm before the storm: there would not be so long a period of steady fellowship under one leader again in the twentieth century.

Not that the church anticipated storms, when in 1979 Berkeley Johnson retired and a new minister was appointed. It was no longer necessary for a minister to work himself into ill-health at the end of his time; Berkeley Johnson retired to a pension, though he did not give up work altogether and took charge of two tiny village churches in Somerset for some years before he

Chapter 2

finally moved away to Nottingham, where he died in 1995. He gave the church due warning of his impending retirement, and the church had plenty of time to consider its new minister.

The man they called was Ernest Pennells, a man who had been in engineering and had just finished his training at Regents Park College. The deacons were unanimous in recommending him, and the church meeting votes were 81.3% in favour. He was inducted in the early September of 1979 and spent some time learning the ropes with Berkeley Johnson before the Johnsons' farewell gathering at the end of the month.

Salem at this time had a hundred and forty-seven members. There was a large group of couples in their thirties and forties, with a sprinkling of younger people and quite a number still who could remember back as far as Walter Holyoak's days. Of course there was a fringe who came to church more from habit than anything else, but there was a strong core of the committed and eager, and these, once the firm hand of Berkeley Johnson was lifted from them, fizzed into life. Ernie Pennells had no difficulty in raising enthusiasm. It was sometimes harder to harness the enthusiasts to work together.

For eighteen months the church made progress. They held a day conference which led to the beginnings of outreach. Groups began to meet for preparation and visiting in the neighbourhood and for practical service. Two ladies of mature years, as well as some young people, asked for baptism. A special church meeting about finance led to greatly increased giving – more in the first half of 1981, they noted, than in the whole of 1980. A Mums and Toddlers group was started. Coffee was served before the morning service. There was a buzz of life and activity that had not been there a year before.

But the storm-clouds were already gathering. To begin with, tensions and differences began to make themselves felt among the membership. Church meetings became long and sometimes heated, and more than once the minister had to speak of their high importance and of the need to listen to the voice of the Holy Spirit. He found it necessary to defend his own timetable, too, to explain how he organised his work and to point out that more of his time spent on one activity would mean less on another. A spirit of criticism was obviously abroad.

And then, in 1981 the storm centre moved to Ernie Pennells' own life. Events occurred there that led to much unhappiness, and early in 1982 he handed in his resignation, left the Baptist ministry altogether and returned to engineering. The church was thrown back on its own resources for the first time for a quarter of a century and had to begin looking for a new pastor.

They had some difficulties in the search. About one prospective minister the membership was divided; another came to see the deacons and both sides were enthusiastic, but God had different plans and before any further action could be taken the man unexpectedly died. However, late in 1982 the members were united in giving an invitation to David Norkett. He had been in the ministry since 1968, but had spent the past thirteen years in Zaire as a missionary. He was a quiet, likeable man. He was inducted in April 1983, and he and the church looked forward to a fruitful partnership.

Once again, there was much to be thankful for in the early part of the new ministry. Some house-groups had already been meeting in an informal way, but David Norkett was convinced of their usefulness and started up five, which flourished. Several people, young and old, were baptised. There was a deacons' retreat, and a church outing, and a coach trip to the 'Mission to London' meeting at Queens Park Rangers stadium. Several times services were held where people could come forward and ask for prayer for healing, which were generally felt to be helpful.

But the problems within the fellowship had not vanished with the coming of a new minister. There were still murmurs of criticism and tensions between individuals. The idea of outreach, which had been shelved with Ernie Pennells' leaving, was approved again, but they found it difficult to know how to get started. Giving was down once more, which was not critical in itself at this point since there were reserves to draw on, but seemed to be symptomatic of a general lack of commitment among the fellowship. There was little sense of joy and assurance, and the minister began to feel as if he was wading through sand.

A small group of deacons was set up to give him support, and they met two or three times a month. David Norkett said that he found this valuable and struggled on into 1984, doing his best to heal rifts, preach the word and

Chapter 2

encourage his people to move beyond themselves. Teams were set up to begin outreach on the 'Good News down the Street' plan, which aimed to make contact with people on the fringe of the church such as the parents of Sunday School children. Suggestions were made that all-age learning groups should be set up to meet during part of the morning service. But neither project really got off the ground. And at the end of 1984 the struggle was too much for this gentle and caring man, and he in his turn resigned, and moved to a pastorate in Hemel Hempstead.

So once again Salem looked for a new minister. Once again they appointed a man and began the ministry with high hopes. But once again the same problems surfaced. Graham Routley was inducted in 1986. He had been trained at Spurgeon's College and had had three pastorates before Salem. He had a clear vision of what might be accomplished for God in this place, and he set about trying to bring it about. But though there were some minor victories he found it an uphill task.

Part of the difficulty was that he wanted to bring about change faster than Salem was ready for it. As generally happens in such a situation there was a large minority who were eager for what they saw as the church reponding to the present needs of the world and who supported the minister, but a not-quite-silent majority, many of them long-standing and faithful members, who did not. In some ways the membership of Salem was quite insular, and those who had worshipped in a set pattern for upwards of thirty years did not find it easy to learn not just new songs but new kinds of songs, or to accept the idea of prayers from the congregation, or of breaking into small groups for prayer in the Sunday services. They were firm in their disapproval of such new-fangled ways, and they extended the disapproval to the minister himself, his preaching, his visiting and his other works.

Salem members have never from the very beginning been a flock of meekly acquiescent sheep. The church was born when individual members followed their own consciences and refused to countenance practices they felt were wrong, and through a century and a half they had followed their pastor faithfully when – but only when – they were convinced that he was God's man giving them God's message. This attitude is a useful check on a pastor and can be an instrument of God's will. But Satan uses the weapons to hand, and in this case the weapons were those same strong wills that might more usefully have been set against himself. Church meetings continued to be long and heated, never lasting less than two hours and sometimes nearer three. Many of the members found them so wearing that they simply stayed away, so that on several occasions there were not enough present to constitute a quorum and no decisions could be taken. The deacons wrestled with the situation and did their best to put things right, but their own group was not united. In the summer of 1989 relations at the deacons' meetings grew so strained and discussions so acrimonious that two deacons resigned. In the autumn of that year Graham Routley was offered a post in East London and under the circumstances he felt that this was a message from the Lord that Salem was no longer the place for him. So in September 1989 Salem received the resignation of its third minister in ten years.

It was clear that things could not go on like this. It was no use simply to invite yet another new minister in the hope that he would miraculously transform the church into a loving, co-operative fellowship. The church would have to take an honest look at itself and take some steps towards the transformation before any new pastorate began. The deacons began the process by standing down and asking that the church should pray very carefully before the new election in April. At the election in 1990 a very small diaconate was formed, just two men who had served before and two women entirely new to the task.

It was a first step, but they were not out of the wood yet. One of the ex-deacons was the treasurer, which made for difficulties when financial decisions were being taken, and this problem was not really resolved until 1993 when he was elected a deacon again. Then there were differences of opinion about a new minister. The church meeting called to consider inviting one man in 1990 was not a happy one. Not only did the votes barely reach the majority needed (the minister declined the invitation for that reason) but when the vote had been taken nearly a third of the members present immediately left the meeting – leaving the rest to infer, rightly or wrongly, that they cared nothing for the other work of the church but had only come to make their

Chapter 2

opinions about the prospective minister known. It was one more symptom of the deeper malaise. A meeting was called with the Area Superintendent, Peter Tongeman, and he suggested a re-dedication service, at which everyone was asked to sign an assurance of repentance and renewed commitment. There were some who resisted – two resigned their membership – but the re-dedication was generally accepted and the church took another step forward.

Satan had not given up the fight. At a meeting in 1991 a stormy exchange on the subject of finance between the moderator, Ewart Graham from Deal, and two members led him to resign the moderatorship, and there had to be more meetings with Peter Tongeman and other officers of the Kent Baptist Association. A new moderator, Alan Dinnie from Willesborough, Ashford, took over, though the brunt of the everyday work still fell on the secretary, David Cook, and his wife. However, with this the tide seemed to have reached its lowest ebb. Throughout this period, in spite of everything there had been good things happening – notably 'Tell Dover', a mission to the town run by the combined Dover churches, and the commissioning of a new leadership team of four Salem members to try to revive and extend the work at Temple Ewell – and despite the tensions and disagreements there was no absolute split in the membership. Several young families left about this time because they moved away to work elsewhere, but the core remained, often unhappy with what was happening but doggedly faithful. And by the beginning of 1992 the area representatives felt that matters were resolved sufficiently for the church to begin to look forward again. Two ministers came to preach but neither felt called to the Salem pastorate. Then towards the end of 1992 David Howells' name came before the deacons. He was then the minister of a church in Chard in Somerset. He was much older than those the church had been considering until now, but that meant that he had experience of twenty-eight years of ministry, so maybe it would not be a bad thing. In January 1993 the church voted unanimously to call him to Salem. When the result was made known it is recorded that they sang the doxology twice, and all the people said 'Amen!'

So through the last seven years of the century the church began the slow process of rebuilding and reuniting the fellowship. If they still felt sometimes

Rev David Howells at his sixtieth birthday party

that they were taking one step forward and two steps back, this was not wholly true. New Bible study groups were started. They met for a prayer workshop and went out into the neighbourhood on 'prayer missions'. David Howells brought to light gifts in unexpected people, and a music group was formed to share the task of playing for the services. People on the fringe of the fellowship came closer in and took part in the life of the church. In 1997 he sent out a call for new deacons, and five were appointed, making a diaconate of ten, the largest for some time. And in particular the worst of the antagonisms had been overcome. Of course members still did not always see eye to eye with each other or with the minister. But on the whole the church grew quietly but steadily stronger.

However, David Howells was not a young man, and his health was not good. In June 1997 he went into hospital for an endoscopy, and later that year he had a heart pacemaker fitted. And the following year his doctor advised him that the effort of full-time ministry was really too much for him. It had been suggested that Andrew Edwards, a member who had come to Salem in 1985 from Canterbury, and who had previously acted as lay pastor to the little church at Aylesham, should become assistant pastor at Salem and help carry some of the burden for him. But it seems that God has never intended Salem to have an assistant pastor. For the fourth time in the church's history the idea of an assistant was barely agreed before it was outdated. David Howells announced that on his doctor's advice he had decided to take early retirement. He left in September 1998 and moved away to Wales, the land of his birth, where with the burden of full-time ministry lifted from him he was

Chapter 2

able to serve God with renewed vigour.

So once more the church was left without a leader, and once more they began the slow process of considering men for the pastorate. Andrew Edwards was willing to take over the lay pastorship of the church, and his experience and insight, as well as those of the moderator, Bob Archer, were a great help as the deacons and leaders considered one after another of the names the Area Superintendent suggested. In 1999 it looked as if a man would be appointed, but though the church called him and he almost accepted, at the last moment he felt that this was not God's will. The church were disappointed and a little indignant. What was happening to them now?

What they could not see was that God had plans for them already in preparation. In 1986 a young man by the name of Nigel Booth and his wife June had attended a baptismal service at Ashford Baptist Church, where one of Salem's own sons, John Hopper, was minister. Within nine months they had come to faith and were baptised themselves, and in 1992 Nigel began church-based training with Spurgeon's College for the Baptist ministry. In 1999 John's wife Judy, hearing that the people of Salem were looking for a minister, thought of Nigel, who was by then pastor of three small churches in Stoke-on-Trent. Contact was made, and church and minister felt that this was God's moving. And in April 2000 Nigel was inducted into the pastorate at Salem.

So the beginning of the new millennium marked the beginning of a new stage in the life of the church. Since his arrival Nigel has taught, encouraged and enthused the people of God at Salem. We have clarified our vision for the work here and begun to implement it. The youth work has been given new heart. Outreach has been started in several areas, including the 'Jesus video' project, a church magazine and web-site, coffee-n-chat mornings and an art and craft group. 'Faith encounter' groups have been held for enquirers and five people have been baptised.

It is clear that Nigel's coming was indeed the will of God. We are going forward with a new impetus, in faith that he who has led us for over a century and a half is leading us still, and will continue so to do.

MEN AND MINISTRIES

Rev Nigel and Mrs June Booth

Chapter 3
Buildings

I**N 1822, when the first 16 members came from Eythorne to plant a church here, Dover was still a small town. It had long outgrown the mediaeval walls that once enclosed it, and only the names, Snargate Street, Cowgate Hill, Townwall Street, remained. By the early 19th century there was building all along the seafront. The old town between the sea and the Maison Dieu was enlarged by a cluster of streets at the western end of the beach called the Pier district, where the harbour trade was carried on. Here the fishermen, sailors, rope-makers, customs officials and the rest lived and worked, the coastal hoys discharged their cargoes, and the Packet boats loaded and unloaded their passengers for France. Up on the Western heights there had been fortifications and on the seafront batteries, with the Grand Shaft connecting the two, since England had been at war with France at the end of the eighteenth century, and the soldiers garrisoned in Dover were still a notable presence in the town.

But it was still a comparatively small place. Much of the modern town had yet to be built. Ladywell was a narrow cobbled alley, what is now Maison Dieu Road a rough lane where produce from the corn mills and market gardens along the river was brought in to feed the town. Folkestone Road ran out past Priory Farm, where later Dover College and the station were to be built, and was immediately between fields. River and Whitfield and even Buckland and Charlton were still self-contained villages and Coombe Valley, Buckland valley and Elms Vale still green with pasture.

Down by the seafront, Snargate Street was – as it continued to be well into the 20th century – a busy throughfare linking the two ends of the town. It was lined on both sides with buildings, tall, narrow premises housing the grocer, the tailor, the shoemaker, the pharmacist, the printer, the bookseller, the jeweller, all cheek by jowl with restaurants, public houses, the Wellington Hall and the Tivoli Theatre. It was an ideally central spot for the new church to meet, and they began gathering in what had been a chemist's shop in Snargate Street itself in 1822.

Between the backs of the Snargate Street shops and the waterfront ran an open space called Commercial Quay. It overlooked what is now called Wellington Dock, the innermost of Dover's harbours, which is also the oldest – first enclosed in Elizabeth I's time and named the Pent. The area along the quay where the commercial shipping unloaded was called Pentside. So when in 1823 the young church raised enough money to build a purpose-made chapel, they bought a piece of land on Commercial Quay, overlooking the water, and the chapel took its name from the area and was known as Pentside Baptist chapel.

The Baptist denomination was by tradition a denomination mainly of village churches, and in the early nineteenth century their places of worship were on the whole plain, unadorned buildings, suitable for the plain, unadorned worship that took place there. Pentside chapel was no exception. Unlike the octagonal meeting house that had been built by the General Baptists (later Unitarians) in Adrian Street in 1820, or the attractive Methodist chapel that would shortly be built in Snargate Street, the Pentside chapel was a flat-faced, rectangular brick building with rows of plain arched windows, standing flush with the other buildings on the quay and looking not unlike a warehouse itself. As the working man passed the chapel on his way from his cramped and chilly home in the Pier district to the marine businesses or the many pubs of the area one wonders whether he was attracted or repelled by its uncompromising facade.

By the end of the 1830s the town was growing fast, and the centre of prosperity was moving east. The commercial traffic still continued in the Pier district, but the Victorian middle class was beginning to make an impact along the seafront and in the centre of the town. Sea air and sea bathing had been discovered to be good for you, and people were coming to Dover for holidays. Several large new hotels had been opened. Terraces of expensive houses had been built along Townwall Street and Waterloo Crescent, where

Chapter 3

the old ropewalk used to be, and a promenade had been surfaced so that the citizens of the town and their visitors could take the air by the sea. The houses and shops along Cannon Street and Biggin Street were expanding to cater for them, and building was extending out along London Road.

The new chapel was to be built in the newer part of the town, and could be expected to attract at least some of the more prosperous of the citizens. The really wealthy would mostly attend the parish churches, but some of the shopkeepers and artisans who made a good profit out of serving them would come to Salem. And overall Baptist outlook was changing. It was no longer considered pretentious to build churches that raised men's thoughts heavenward. The new chapel of 1839 was a much more elegant building than the old Pentside chapel. It had the classical facade that was becoming popular. It was, said the church to the Association in the year it was opened, 'neat, elegant and attractive, without needless display or anything which a sound taste would condemn'.

Inside it followed the practice widespread in the early nineteenth century of providing box pews that families could consider their own, with high sides that stopped attention from wandering and a door that had to be unlocked each Sunday morning by the pew-opener. For this privilege they paid rent, which was one of the mainstays of the minister's stipend. The pews were square in section and extremely uncomfortable, but of course one did not go to church to be comfortable.

Baptists recognise three ordinances, baptism, communion, and the preaching of the word, and the front of the chapel was accordingly taken up by baptistry, communion table and pulpit. The positions of the three indicate their relative importance to that early congregation.

The baptistry was a rectangular tank about four feet deep sunk in the floor at the centre, in front of the pews. It was surrounded by a rail and was probably always covered by boards when not in use. For a baptism it would be opened and filled and the candidate went down the steps at the side and into the water to be immersed by the minister. In 1840 it would have been filled with cold water, though one hopes the caretaker might have been instructed at least to add a few kettles-full of boiling water just before the service began to take the chill off for the candidates. Later there was a boiler to provide warm water, and later still an electric immersion heater.

Over the covered baptistry normally stood the communion table. It stood at the front of the church all the time, but was only covered with its cloth, plates and cup for the communion service itself. From within the high box pews it must have been almost invisible.

But the most important of the three ordinances to that early congregation was the preaching of the word. The pulpit was not only central but lifted up so that even from within the pews the preacher was clearly visible. Exactly what the original pulpit was like we do not know; it was altered more than once over the years. In 1861 it was draped with black to mark the death of the Prince Consort. It was a feature in itself, and there never seems to have been any decoration on the wall above or around it - though much later, in 1920, there was a suggestion that a text should be painted there at the expense of one of the members. This was not received with enthusiasm by the rest of the church, who suggested that if he wanted to put a text on a wall the school hall might be a better place for it. He withdrew his offer.

The one problem associated with the pulpit was that of making the preacher's voice heard throughout the church. Unaided by modern technology, the minister had to project his voice like an actor or risk half his congregation not hearing him, and churches were not designed like theatres. The difficulty was intensified by a persistent echo, and though various efforts were made to eradicate them the problems continued throughout the history of the building and were not really cured until the advent of microphones in the nineteen fifties.

The building was lighted by gas, which had reached the main streets of Dover in 1822. Music was provided by an organ, probably always situated at the back of the church. It was pumped in those early days by hand, and

> ‘May he who dwells between the cherubim shine upon all our services in the new place ’   *Church Minutes August 1840*

CHAPTER 3

> ❛A parchment bearing an inscription to the following effect was enclosed in a bottle and placed in the [foundation] stone [of the chapel in Biggin street]
> To God alone be glory.
> This stone (the first of a new edifice intended for the worship of a christian church, for the preaching of the everlasting gospel, and for the promotion of the Divine honour) was laid by Mr Alfred Kingsford on the 20th of April 1840.
> Pastor of the Church — the Revd. J.P Hewlett
> Deacons — Messrs Alfred Kingsford & William Pepper
> Architect — Mr Frank Height
> Builder — Mr Joseph Stff❜ *(Church Minutes April 1840)*

'organ-blower' was a recognised appointment for many years. (It is tempting to speculate that the traditional 'hymn-sandwich' form of Baptist worship – hymn, reading, hymn, prayer, hymn, sermon – was developed as much to give the organ-blower a rest between efforts as for any liturgical reason.)

The chapel of 1839 was set a little back from the road, so that in front of it there was a grassy space about 40 feet wide and 30 feet from pavement to wall. At this time there were no municipal cemeteries: all burials took place in the graveyard or crypt belonging to a church. Most of Dover's dissenting chapels had their graveyard attached and Salem's little garden soon began to be used as a burial ground. Between 1840 and 1850 twenty-eight people were buried there, many of them children. The first one, a child called Elizabeth Smith, was laid to rest in July 1840, before the chapel was even in use. A vault was also constructed under the ground near the road. Around the end of this period the authorities began to be increasingly concerned about the state of the nation's graveyards, especially in the growing towns where there really wasn't room for all the new graves that were needed, and in the early 1850s the Municipal Burials Act was passed and cemeteries were provided on the outskirts of towns, where people of any persuasion or none could be buried. In Dover all the graveyards of the borough except St Mary's

Salem chapel as built in 1840

New Cemetery (Cowgate) were closed in 1853. In any case Salem's little graveyard was by then almost full, and the last recorded burial there was at the end of Hewlett's ministry, in 1850.

Seating for four hundred people must have seemed wildly optimistic to the little church that built the chapel in 1840, but it was not many years before they had to begin to consider whether it would be possible to enlarge it. There had been a schoolroom attached to the back of the chapel from the beginning. Around 1857 they had for a while a particularly energetic and enthusiastic Sunday School Superintendent, E. L. Williams, who cajoled teachers and friends into giving £145 with which to build another room above that one, which was then available for such events as 'public tea meetings' as well as Sunday School classes. (When E. L. Williams moved away from the town they gave him a silver-plated inkstand in recognition of all his efforts.) In 1845 a small bequest was left specifically towards the erection of a gallery in the body of the chapel, but somehow the money was needed for other things, and although still officially available it had actually been borrowed for other uses long before the plan came to fruition.

But in 1879 the two people came together who would make it happen. Elijah Edwards had overseen the building of a new chapel at his previous pastorate in Redruth, and knew it could be done. And the railway contractor T. A. Walker not only had the experience to carry it out but was willing to make a large contribution to its cost. (It has been suggested that he also used spare material from his work for the building, whose iron girders always had a certain air of the railway station about them.) In 1879 the plan was brought before the church and by 1880 the alterations were complete.

They were considerable. The sanctuary itself had galleries added on three

Chapter 3

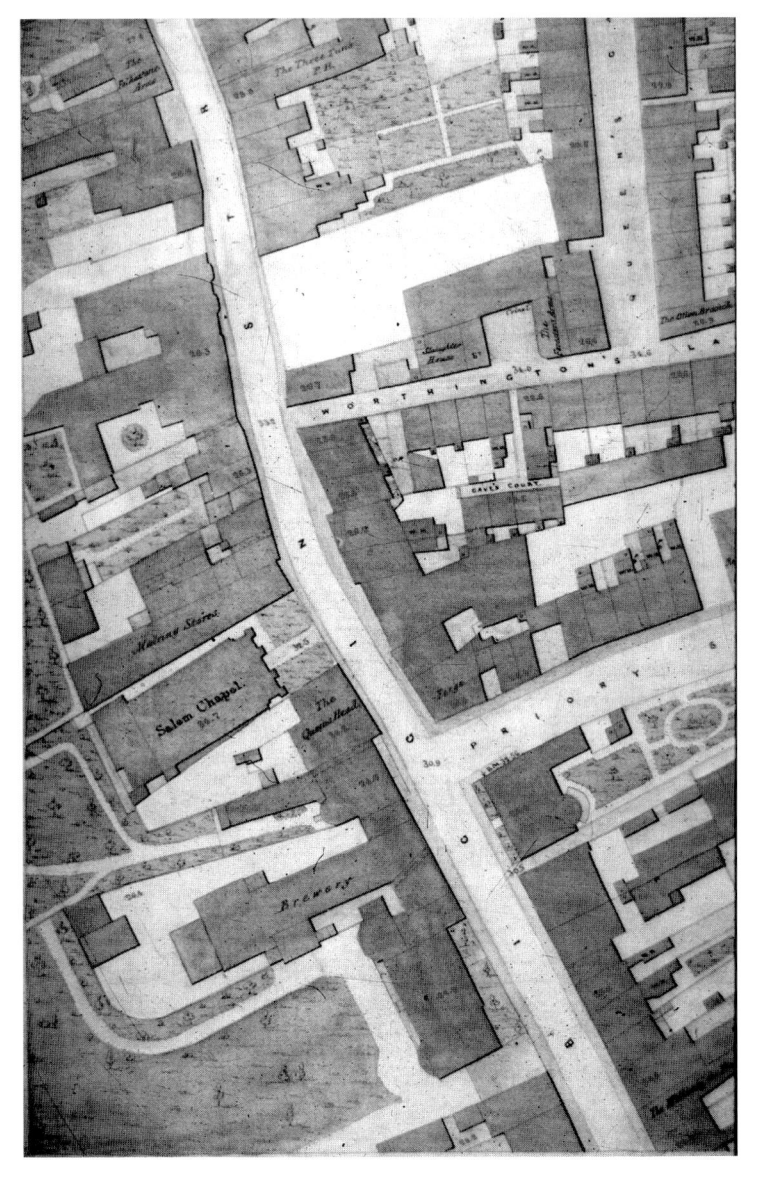

Plan of part of Dover in 1852. Salem chapel is set back from the road, with the graveyard in front. [photo courtesy of Dover Museum]

sides. Downstairs the old box pews were altered to make more comfortable open pews. It must have been an amazing experience to go into the altered building for the first time and feel yourself surrounded above and below by ranks of visible worshippers.

The front of the building was brought forward. As the century passed the church was becoming involved in many new activities as well as attracting an ever larger congregation, and extra space was needed on weekdays as well as Sundays. So a lobby was created in front, with stairs leading up from it to the galleries and classrooms on either side. Above the lobby was a big new lecture hall. Building forward like this, of course, meant building over the old graveyard, and the Home Secretary had to be approached for permission. It is not recorded that any of the members objected to walking on the tombs of their forefathers, but they did not want to lose sight of the gravestone of George Leach, a respected member who had died of tuberculosis in 1848 and would still have been remembered by many, and the stone was moved to an honourable place in the new lobby.

The new exterior was more ornate than the original – the Dover Express in 1896 called it 'a handsome Grecian frontage' – and many Dovorians will remember how it dominated that part of Biggin Street. No-one of that day worried about any difficulty the elderly or disabled might find in negotiating the steps that led up from the pavement to the big double doors.

What did concern them as time went on was the difficulty of ventilating the church, which might now have six hundred people and the gas lights all generating heat and competing for air, and several attempts were made at various times to get enough air into the building, none altogether successful. Over the years the heating was improved and so was the lighting. Then in 1900 came a dramatic change: three friends offered to pay the cost of having electric light installed. The offer was gratefully accepted, though they didn't get carried away: the lights seem to have been installed at first only over the centre of the church and were switched off during the sermon. Gradually the members got used to the new system and voted to leave them on for the whole service, and then to light the galleries and passage. In 1931 it was suggested that the electricity should be used to install an electric blower to

Chapter 3

Salem chapel after its enlargement in 1880

The interior of the Biggin Street chapel in 1913 [photo by Charles Harris]

the organ, but several members were doubtful. If there were variations in the supply might they not damage the organ? They were reassured that 'the Law covers us against any charges consequent upon a change in the nature of Dover's electric supply'.

Biggin Street was widened in the 1880s and Dover became only the second town in the country to run trams for its citizens. The tram route ran past the front of the chapel and there was a stop outside the door, which must have been very handy for those who lived beyond comfortable walking distance.

By the early years of the new century the two schoolrooms at the back of the building were sixty years old, cramped, dingy and in bad repair. And the National Sunday School Union was insisting on the importance of dividing children up into classes and teaching them according to age, which was next to impossible with three hundred children in two rooms. Once again a new young minister – this time Walter Holyoak – arrived, looked at the accommodation and found it wanting, and the church plunged into the business

CHAPTER 3

of raising the money needed to build a whole new block. The first stone was laid in 1909, and a bottle placed in a cavity with a shilling and Baptist journals of the day inside. The buildings were opened, with tea and services, in June 1910. The final cost was nearly £4500.

It was an age for church-building. In Dover the Congregational church (now United Reformed), London Road Methodist church, and St Martin's and St Barnabas' C of E (the latter now demolished) were all built between 1901 and 1903, and in 1910 the Methodist chapel was opened at the bottom of Folkestone Road. But even compared with the new churches these Sunday School buildings were no mean achievement. From the back of the chapel, beyond a lobby and two vestries, ran a hall fifty feet long, with four classrooms opening off it on each side and a kitchen. Set apart from the main block along a covered way there was also a small two-storey block, the Infants' and Junior rooms. In fact there had been even more ambitious plans, to put a gallery in the hall and to include a caretaker's cottage, to roof with sheet lead, and to heat with hot water pipes instead of gas radiators, all of which eventually had

The opening of the new school hall in 1910 [photo by Charles Harris]

to be abandoned because of the cost. Nevertheless they might be justly proud of the new block when it was opened, and the rooms were very well used for half a century and more – not only by the church itself but by the local authorities in two world wars and by the Girls' School when they needed extra accommodation from 1931 to 1935.

The lane along the side of the building came into public use for the first time with the opening of these buildings and the council accepted the church's suggestion that it should be named after their late revered pastor. It is still called Edwards Road, sharing with Taverner's Lane (now vanished) the distinction of being called after prominent Dover Baptists.

Salem was not extensively damaged during the war, and the government compensation scheme covered what repairs were needed. There was other damage in Biggin Street, however, and the Town Council considered issuing a compulsory purchase order on Salem and rebuilding the whole of that block. Perhaps they took into account the alarm and indignation of Salem's people at the suggestion; at any rate they reconsidered and though the stretch between Edwards Lane and the Town Hall was rebuilt, Salem was safe.

It was in the first years of Berkeley Johnson's ministry that letters began to arrive asking if the church would be interested in selling the site. By now Dover, with a population of over forty thousand, had spread out and engulfed the valleys and villages that surrounded it. Two wars and an immense increase in cross-channel traffic had altered the seafront out of recognition. The Pier district had been virtually obliterated, along with the seaward side of Snargate Street and Commercial Quay. The rest of Snargate Street was cut off from the town and had become a backwater. Supermarkets and multiple stores had taken over most of the old family businesses in Cannon Street and Biggin Street, and were wanting to expand further. Space there was at a premium.

The chapel, parts of it more than a hundred years old now, was familiar and beloved, but it was expensive to heat and difficult to clean. There were rats in the passage and cockroaches in the kitchen, and the roof needed costly repairs. For all but the faithful few church-going on Sundays had given way to family outings, and congregations now rarely filled the downstairs pews, let alone the galleries. And the motor car had arrived. Few of the members

CHAPTER 3

lived close to the town centre any more: many came in by car from Maxton or Whitfield or River and when they arrived there was nowhere close to the church for them to park.

No-one concerned with town planning seems to have objected to the demolition of a building with so honourable a history. It was bought by Boots the Chemists and pulled down without ceremony, though the front of their new shop had to be built slightly back from the line of the rest of the street because the vault and its graves still stood under the pavement. Five memorial tablets were rescued before demolition and set in the wall inside the new building, but the gravestone of George Leach and the carefully deposited documents in the foundations seem to have been lost for ever.

The church looked at several sites before settling on the one in Maison Dieu Road. The one they eventually chose has its disadvantages: it is out of the pedestrian area so few people pass it on foot, and for drivers coming along the busy road it is difficult to see until too late. However it is in a pleasant situation, away from the bustle of the centre but only a few minutes' walk from buses and shops, and the front of the church looks up towards the castle. The new buildings are on one level throughout with the church at one side of a vestibule and a large hall and kitchen at the other, and a smaller hall and other rooms at the back. They are attractively laid out, with garden plots

---

Deacons in 1972 when the new building was erected:

Priscilla Cocker *Hospital matron*
Elsie Pascall *Married lady*
Jack Connor *Travel agent*
C. Roy Mackrow *Retired bank manager*
Jack Cook *Retired Post Office inspector*
David Cook *Post Office executive officer*
Arthur Clipsham *British Telecom executive officer*
Oliver Hoskin *Director of Castle Concrete*
Robert Wheeler *Gas Board surveyor*
Leslie Taylor *Retired missionary*

The erection of the new building in Maison Dieu Road [photo by E. Weaver and D. Cook]

surrounding a good-sized car-park at the front, and are generally much admired.

Since the war the fashion in church building had changed, and churches were no longer being designed with a nave full of pews looking up to the altar or the pulpit, and dark wood and stained glass making the interior cool and dim and reverent. Both Anglican and Nonconformist churches of the fifties and sixties were bright and airy, with light-coloured fittings and plenty of room for movement. Salem's sanctuary is square rather than rectangular in plan, with a centre aisle and wide pews angled at the sides to emphasise the oneness of the family and the priesthood of all believers. The pulpit still stands at the centre of the front wall but is no longer raised so high above the pews. The communion table stands in front of the pulpit, and there is space around it for today's minister to come down and chat informally to the children or congregation, or for members to lead prayers from the microphones there. There was discussion over whether to have the baptistry in the centre or at

CHAPTER 3

the side of the church; it was eventually decided to put it at the side but to leave it open to remind people of its significance. Unfortunately an open baptistry is easy to fall into, and when in 1996 a lady arranging flowers did just that a cover was made for it when it was not in use.

Naturally the new buildings were not taken over without problems. It was perhaps no-one's fault that the holes set in the front of the pews for the communion glasses were almost exactly the size of a new penny, but the fact was soon discovered with glee by a generation of Sunday School children who dropped their collection pennies into them, and with exasperation by the teachers who then had to get them out. Nor could the church of the sixties really be blamed for not looking forward twenty-five years to the time when the single organ began to give way to a group of musicians with varied instruments, and so not allowing space enough for a dozen people (on special occasions) to sit in the 'music corner' between the pulpit and the wall.

There were problems, though, which might have been foreseen and

Inside the new building, at the induction of Nigel Booth in 2000
[photo D. Oram]

prevented. The flat roof did not let water escape easily, which led to decay and rain leaking through, and it had to be re-covered twice in the next thirty years. And there were serious difficulties with the heating system. For years the sanctuary and the large hall were always cold, even though the other rooms might be stifling. Repeated attempts were made to put things right but to no avail. In 1977 an independent heating consultant was called in and the architect eventually agreed that the system was inadequate and paid £1000 towards improvements, with £1000 costs. The improvements were made; this went a good way towards putting things right, but it was still not a hundred per cent satisfactory, and at the time of writing the boiler room is still on the roof and the boilers still go out quite frequently, so that someone has to climb up on a Sunday morning and re-light them for the church to be warm in time for the service.

The new building cost a total of £67,000. Most of this was covered by the sale of the old building, though some had to be borrowed from the Baptist Union. Despite the many little early faults that seemed to take for ever to put right, the church has been very pleased with its new buildings. For those who like to feel that the past is not totally lost there are a number of things in the building that were kept from old Salem, with their histories attached. The memorial tablets are set in the wall. There is an armchair made from wood from a tree planted by William Carey, that was given to the Sunday School by Mr and Mrs Jarry in 1910, and one of the communion trays was given in Mrs Harris in 1920 in memory of her husband. The big silver offering plate was given to Salem after the second world war when the Daystar Mission in Princes Street closed. Even the ballot box still used in elections of ministers and deacons was made and given by one of the church members, Joe Page, in 1951.

Some still have wistful memories of the big halls and many classrooms of the old building, and the central position that meant singing carols on the steps and throwing open the doors to passers-by. But the new building is clean, attractive and convenient. A new generation knows nowhere else. In 2001 two young members were married in the church whose parents were married there in 1975. The place changes but the family goes on.

Chapter 4

Church organisation, association and worship

A BAPTIST church is an independent unit, a gathering of people who believe in the central tenets of the Christian faith and in particular in the importance of believers' baptism. Unlike the Anglicans, Methodists or Presbyterians, the Baptists have no central body which exercises authority over all the local churches. Each church is autonomous: it calls its own leader and is responsible under God for its own finance, buildings, discipline and form of worship. There is, though, a strong family likeness in the traditions of the local fellowships, so that Salem's story reflects that of many other Baptist churches.

Except for short periods between ministries the Salem church has always had a full-time, paid minister. Most of these men, though not all, were trained at one of the Bible Colleges. Their title has varied; for a good part of the church's life the leader has been called the Pastor – the shepherd. The alternative name is minister, one who serves. With the exception of Captain Passingham in 1871 they all accepted the title Reverend in written documents, though not normally in speech.

The pastor is supported in his leadership by a body of deacons. This was the practice from the very early days, though no minutes have survived of their early meetings. Such meetings must have taken place, but perhaps they were just informal conversations without minutes: the regular monthly deacons' meeting is first mentioned in 1855. The number of deacons has varied over the years. At first there were just two, William Pepper and Alfred Kingsford, though a few years later they had four 'assistants' to help them in the 'temporal affairs of the church' such as dealing with pew rents. In 1845 the growing church decided to appoint five more deacons. Their procedure is interesting. It all happened at a single meeting. A number of men were proposed and seconded for the office, and then the names were taken in the order in which they were proposed and a simple vote was taken on each. Once the five places were filled the election was finished. They felt that a secret ballot was unscriptural, and perhaps it is not surprising that the five chosen men were all elected unanimously. They chose five 'to prevent the necessity of another choice for many years', so clearly there was no set term of office.

When Passingham came to be pastor of the church, among his other innovative ideas he felt strongly that, according to the practice of the early church, the leaders of the church should be called elders. There seems to have been no particular distinction between elders as leaders for spiritual matters and deacons for material matters; there is a fleeting mention of both elders and deacons elected together in 1873, but after that we only hear of elders. They were so called all through Passingham's and Elijah Edwards' ministries; then when Walter Holyoak took over the church reverted to the original name, and the leaders have been called deacons ever since. At that time it was also agreed that the deacons should be elected to serve for three years and then must be re-elected. This is how things still are, but in 1911 it became possible for a man who had served for at least fifteen consecutive years to become a life deacon.

In 1918 a small upheaval occurred, when Miss Winterbourn's name was put forward as a nomination for the diaconate. The pastor gently explained that the church rules did not allow women deacons. However, he said, the rules might be changed, and in July 1920 changed they were, and the maximum number of deacons became: nine men, three women and one life deacon of

> ‘Reported: A gift of a second-hand bath chair received . . . for use of which by members of the Church and Congregation no charge would be made.’ *August 1918*

CHAPTER 4

The deacons with Mr and Mrs Holyoak 1920s

either sex. The idea of having a woman deacon seems to have thrown the church into quite a flurry. Normally the deacons made their own nominations first and then members could put forward other names, but at the first AGM after the change there were no nominations at all for women from the diaconate but seven from the members, including Miss Winterbourn and, perhaps surprisingly, Mrs Holyoak. Three of the nominees promptly withdrew, and when the election was taken only one of the remaining four had a high enough majority – not in fact Miss Winterbourn but a Mrs Pratt, who became Salem's first woman deacon. Since then the specific numbers have been dropped and now any combination of male and/or female deacons, to a

> 'Duties of women deacons:
> representing the church at funerals
> visiting the sick
> assisting on baptismal occasions
> welcoming women strangers
> visiting candidates [for baptism]
> attending deacons meetings'
>
> *(Church Minutes 1920)*

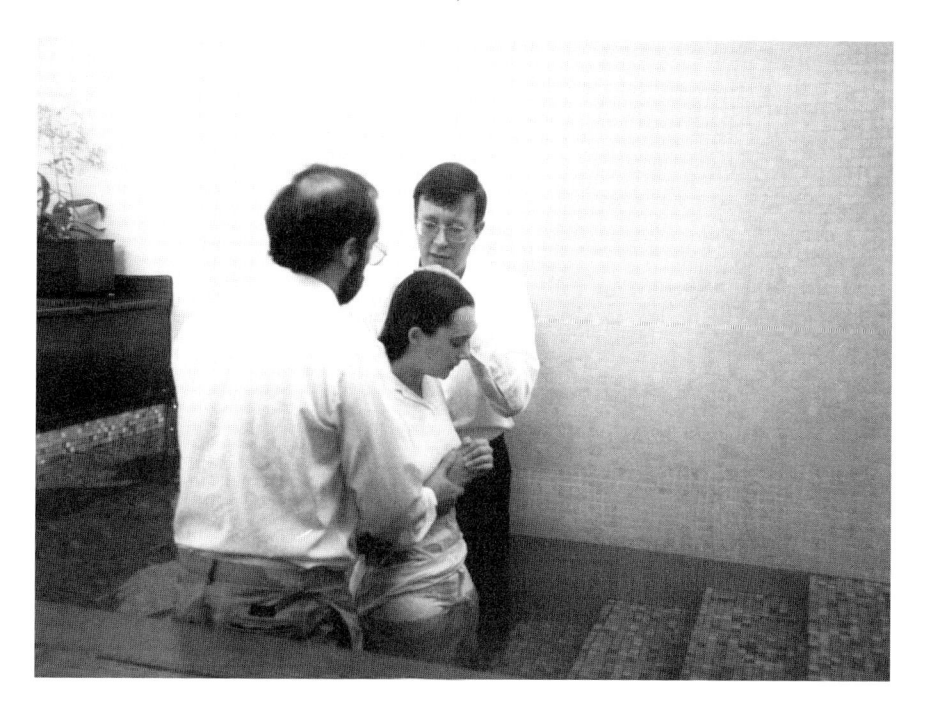

Baptism of Fiona Edwards, autumn 2000 [photo – June Booth]

maximum of twelve, is acceptable.

Membership of a Baptist church normally follows baptism: when a person gives his allegiance to Christ he affirms this by baptism and then is received into the local church. This has always been the practice at Salem. Sometimes baptism is not possible because of age or illness or for some other reason, and all the ministers have been willing to accept a profession of faith without baptism in particular circumstances, but they have differed in what circumstances they would accept. Nowadays a baptism is almost always part of a regular Sunday service, but it was not always so. In the early days the standard report in the minutes says that, 'So-and-so was received into membership and baptised the following Wednesday'. This would have been at a special evening meeting, where people from other churches could be invited without taking them away from their own fellowship on a Sunday.

CHAPTER 4

Once received into the church, all members have a right and a duty to attend the church meeting, where the spiritual and material business of the church is considered and decided. It is the church as a whole and not the pastor or the deacons who have the responsibility for making decisions. The church meeting may appear to an outsider to have a good deal in common with, say, a Trade Union meeting, but this appearance is deceptive. Though votes are taken and acted upon, the church should be seeking not the will of the majority but the will of God on the matters before it, and mostly it is so. Although over the years there have been occasions of dispute and disagreement – and, it has to be said, subsequent anger and resentment – there have also been occasions like the meeting of 1846 after which the secretary wrote, 'The doxology was sung with peculiar feelings of gratitude to God for the peaceful and orderly way in which the business of this evening has been carried on, and the satisfactory result in which it has terminated.'

In practice many minor matters are decided by the deacons alone, and all major items will normally have been considered first by the deacons so that

---

Trustees of rear premises of Salem 1904

Henry Foster (of Clapham Common) *retired Trinity pilot*
Allan Macdougall *retired Customs Officer*
Charles Edward Ashdown (of Bournemouth) *Paper manufacturer*
Edward George Chapman *retired leather seller*
George Charles Spain *Confectioner*
Thomas Wyborn Denne *Trinity pilot*
William Garland *Temperance hotel proprietor*
William Bradley *Corn merchant*
Frederick Bosworth Kingsford *Gentleman*
John Farley Foord *Foreman boiler maker*
James Cambridge Young - *Bootmaker*

(Trust deed of ground in rear of Chapel 1904)

> 'It being a stormy night the members present were few, namely the Pastor, Deacons Barling and Scott and ten other members.'
> (Church Minutes 20th August 1931)

they can recommend a course of action to the members. It can be difficult for the minister to tread a wise path between allowing the members so much voice in the meeting that time is wasted in irrelevancies and allowing so little that they feel they have had no say in what is decided. Many may feel that there is little point in turning out on a cold, wet night simply to ratify decisions that have virtually been already made by the pastor and deacons. Perhaps for this reason it has often been difficult over the years to persuade people to attend, and it is interesting to see that the number at church meetings bears very little relation to the number on the roll. (See appendix, page 149). Even when the total membership was over three hundred there were rarely more than fifty at a church meeting, often no more than thirty and occasionally even fewer. Various strategies have been tried to encourage people to attend. Meetings have at different times been held monthly, bi-monthly or quarterly. They have followed the evening prayer meeting or they have been combined with a tea. In 1963 a quorum was introduced so that unless a quarter of the total membership was present no business could be done – and in fact on several occasions in the low period of the nineteen eighties the quorum was not reached and either the meeting was abandoned or discussion was allowed but decisions had to wait till the next meeting.

Any Other Business is first recorded in the minutes in 1945. At its best Any Other Business can be an opportunity for an individual member to share with the rest matters close to his heart, and thus used it may be the very voice of God speaking to the church. At its worst it can be a theatre for aggrieved members to bring up matters which they cannot make heard anywhere else, matters in fact which they know would, if put to their properly appointed diaconate, be dismissed out of hand. When Ernie Pennells took over the church meeting in 1979 he wanted to reject AOB altogether and insist that any business must be brought to the deacons or the pastor before the meeting and put formally on the agenda. This was not well received, and a compromise was reached by which any matter for AOB must be recorded at the beginning of the meeting so that at least the chairman had a chance to consider it before it was introduced later. This rule is still in force; happily in a united church it is seldom necessary to apply it.

The main gathering of the church, of course, has always been the Sunday service, where God's people come together to worship him. In the very early days the Sunday services and a prayer meeting and 'lecture' were virtually the only activities of the church. Later many other organisations were formed as the church tried in different ways to attract people or to reach out to help them, but the worship service was still the one place where all the members and many who were not members came together each week. In the early days there were three services each Sunday, at 'a quarter before eleven, at half past two and half past six'. By the end of the century the afternoon service had been abandoned, and the morning service moved to the standard Nonconformist time of eleven o'clock. In 1989 it was suggested that the morning service should be moved to half past ten; there was some resistance, but the new time was tried for six months and was never changed back.

There is nothing to tell us what Salem's early services were like, but there was almost certainly congregational singing, extempore prayer from the pulpit, Bible readings and a sermon. Whether others besides the minister took part we do not know but probably the only congregational participation was the singing. By the early years of the twentieth century there was an occasional venture into drama, but it was not until the nineteen seventies that, as a new desire spread across the denomination to involve the congregation more fully in worship, members began sometimes to take a larger part, praying, reading the Bible or coming forward to explain matters of importance for people's giving or prayer. More recently still there have been unusual services led by or for the young people in which dance, drama or games have been brought out of the Sunday School and made part of the service of worship.

The sermon has been at the centre of Nonconformist worship ever since the Reformation. The two hour sermons of the early days had grown shorter by the nineteenth century, but without a set liturgy it was still the heart of the service, the point at which the Bible came alive, when the people heard God encouraging, commanding, comforting or chiding through the mouth of his servant the minister. A minister might be judged on his sermons; one of the points at issue between Alfred Ibberson and his deacons was the poor quality of his preaching.

Singing at services has a more patchy heritage. The use of hymns and 'spiritual songs' goes back to the New Testament, but when the Reformation church diverged from the state and tried to distinguish between those at a service who had made a commitment to Christ and those who were merely interested spectators, difficulties arose. There was argument on the subject in the meetings of the early Baptist associations, some feeling that to ask the uncommitted among the congregation to sing words expressing worship that they did not truly believe was asking them to act a lie. However, by the time Salem was built this was in the past, and clearly this church sang from the beginning. In the early days the lines of the hymns were read out for the congregation to follow, a common practice at a time when many members would have been more or less illiterate. After a few years a Particular Baptist hymnbook called *A New Selection* was introduced. Later they used one edited

Choir outing 1913

Chapter 4

by Spurgeon, called *Our Own Hymn Book,* and then in 1904 changed to the *Baptist Church Hymnal* (BCH). Each time a new book was introduced people complained about having to learn the new hymns, or new tunes to the old words, and the old Sankey book *Sacred Songs and Solos*, with its popular, catchy tunes, lingered on for use in the chapels and the evening meetings long after it had been banished from the regular Salem services. The BCH was followed by the *Baptist Hymn Book,* but by the time the new *Baptist Praise and Worship* was brought out in 1991 Salem had moved sideways to using *Mission Praise*. Recently popular Christian music has been flowing off the pens of the musicians so fast that it is hard to keep up with, and an overhead projector and a copyright licence have become a standard part of many churches' equipment, so that the church can sing the latest songs without having to buy too many copies of new music which may only stay in fashion for a year or two.

Soon after the church began they formed a choir, which sat in the front two pews to encourage the singing of the congregation. By 1872 when Captain Passingham took over clearly the singing at services had become one of the casualties of the general decline. A new member called Mr Dimmock wanted to begin a singing class and Passingham agreed, though with a certain reluctance. How long this class lasted we do not know. After that there was no regular choir until 1908. Perhaps the singing at the services in Elijah Edwards' time needed no improvement. However, with the introduction of the BCH the singing at services became less than confident again, and a

> 'Mr Freegard referred to the singing at the morning Communion service . . . It was decided to appeal to friends to sit nearer the front . . . ' *Church Minutes November 1908)*
>
> 'Mr Freegard . . . recommended the retention of some of the old tunes instead of those in the Hymnal at the Sunday services ' *(Church Minutes January 1908)*

Singing group Christmas 1997 [photo D. Oram]

committee recommended the formation of a new singing class. Its aims at the beginning were modest: to practise the tunes in the new church hymnal and to prepare 'a cantata or service of song', but not to sing anthems except on special occasions. However, the choir which was formed then lasted, with breaks during the wars, until the nineteen sixties. As well as leading the singing on Sundays they presented a cantata each year – in some years two – sang anthems at public meetings such as the Armistice Day celebrations, sent a group on more than one occasion to join the united male voice choirs at the Albert Hall, and had their own social calendar with outings and parties. It was not until Berkeley Johnson's time that, with a smaller membership and with singing no longer taught in schools, the choir eventually began to fail. It closed down not long before the church moved to the new building, and since then groups of singers have been called together to lead worship on special occasions only.

The principles of the Reformation also affected Baptist worship in the way the communion service was celebrated. All Salem members were expected to take communion regularly. Registers were kept to check how often they did so, and anyone absent for a prolonged period without good reason could be erased from the church roll. As late as the nineteen sixties members were issued with a sheet of dated tickets which were torn off and placed in the offering plate at the communion service so that the deacons could check who was there. But in a Baptist church the congregation were rarely all members and therefore could not all be assumed to be believers, and it was very important to the church that only believers took communion – so important, in fact, that more than once in the early days admission tickets were issued and attendance at communion was by ticket only. At an ordinary Sunday service they expected uncommitted worshippers as well, so at Salem as in most Baptist churches the communion was celebrated in an extra service following the main service. Until the second half of the twentieth century the two were separated by a few minutes' pause when those not intending to take communion could quietly leave. The frequency and timing of the communion service have varied over the years, from once a month in the early days to every week in the 1870s, and then settling into the present pattern. Now the communion is not separated, but is part of the ordinary service, celebrated once at the end of a morning and once at the end of an evening service each month.

When the church was formed, the custom was for the wine to be passed round to the worshippers in a single cup. The wine in the cup would have been ordinary fermented wine and no-one would have had any objection to this. The young temperance movement was concentrating its attention on the drinking of spirits; wine or beer was the normal drink with meals, considerably safer than the water of the day. (This also explains how the owner of a brewery came to be so prominent in Salem's early life, a fact which must have been something of an embarrassment to a later generation.) However, when at the end of the century the Nonconformist churches became deeply committed to the temperance cause, and the movement itself widened its objectives to include all alcoholic drinks, it was obviously inconsistent for the churches to use wine for communion, and it became usual to use unfermented grape juice. This in turn meant that the cup, used by all the communicants and no longer sterilised to some extent by the alcohol, was perceived to be a health hazard, and churches began to change to taking the wine in individual glasses.

At Salem the use of individual cups was suggested in 1918. When the suggestion was brought forward it was not received with universal approval and they decided to have a year's trial, using the common cup at one service and individual cups at the other service each month. This plan was a little delayed when they discovered the war-time cost of the small cups, but eventually, after one tray had been donated by a member in memory of her husband, they used them for the first time in 1920. The year of trial stretched into six years. At each AGM they voted on which the members preferred and each time there was a significant minority who did not want to change so the alternate usage continued. At last, in 1926, they decided to offer both the one and the individual cups at each service, and eventually – perhaps when a generation of traditionalists had passed on – the individual cups only were used and the large cup was merely placed symbolically in the centre of the table. In 1980 murmurs were heard that perhaps a shared loaf was also unhygienic, but these were overcome fairly quickly and Salem continues to use one loaf, the participants breaking off a piece as it is offered to them.

Although it organises itself and is responsible only to God and its own members, a Baptist church does not stand alone. From the very early days of Baptist life the churches came together in local associations, and early in the nineteenth century the Baptist Union was formed to help individual churches and associations to work together.

The new church applied to join the local association in 1839 while they were still meeting in Military Road. Over a century and a half that association has been variously the East Kent, the East Kent and Sussex, the Kent and Sussex and the Kent Baptist Association – and is at present in the process of changing again – but the church has been a member of the association, whatever area it covered, for almost all that time. They took their membership seriously and were not slow to criticise when they felt it necessary; in 1848 they left the association 'on account of its utter inefficiency'. In 1857 they

Chapter 4

Kent and Sussex Baptist Association Assembly meeting at Salem 1915

had rejoined but were remarking critically in their annual letter that the churches needed to 'take up the cross, not ape the world's expensive customs'. But they remained members, and over the years have contributed much to the life of the association. Each year they have sent representatives to the annual meeting and five times (in 1843, 1880, 1915, 1953 and 1974) that meeting has been held at Salem. Seven Salem ministers have held the post of Moderator of the Association, and Elijah Edwards and Walter Holyoak were Association Secretaries. For its part the Association has given support, advice and sometimes financial aid, beginning in 1839 when they sent officers to advise during the split from Pentside and continuing as late as 1990 when they sent officers to advise in the domestic upheavals taking place then at Salem.

The national body, the Baptist Union, is by its nature farther removed from the local church. Though delegates have been sent whenever possible to attend the annual Assembly and report back to the church what is happening nationally, when Assemblies have been held in distant parts of the country it has not always been possible. The church has used many of the BU's publications, though, and has contributed generously over the years to the Baptist Missionary Society and Home Mission which are administered by the Union. Berkeley Johnson was from 1973 to 1992 Secretary to the national Baptist Building Fund.

As well as associating with the wider Baptist community, the church at Salem has always had contact with other Christians closer to home. At first this contact was with like-minded Nonconformists, but during the twentieth century we have moved more and more into fellowship with the other denominations. At the end of the nineteenth century the free churches of Dover were uniting to hold evangelistic campaigns, and in 1896 the Free

Christians Together in Dover. Good Friday Procession of Witness, 1990s.
[photo D. Oram]

Chapter 4

Church Council was set up. From 1903 it issued a magazine, the Dover and District Free Churchman, and organised events such as missions, an annual exchange of preachers, the showing of the Billy Graham film and a meeting at the town hall on the day of George V's coronation. More recently this body has enlarged to include the majority of the Christian churches in the town and became the Dover Christian Council and then, more simply, Christians Together in Dover. Once again it issues a magazine, the Dover Christian Chronicle, to the member churches, and organises events such as the annual Procession of Witness through the town on Good Friday, and outreach such as 'Tell Dover', the united mission in Pencester Gardens in 1991, and the 'Jesus video' distribution in 2001.

Salem is still a member of all three associations. The task of proclaiming the gospel has not changed since 1839, and God's people must work together at it.

Chapter 5
Salem's associated chapels

UNTIL the nineteenth century England was a land of villages. With the exception of London the towns were small, and the vast majority of the people worked on the land and lived in little settlements of perhaps a few hundred people. Until the coming of the railways such villages were quite isolated; a farmer and his wife might take an hour's journey to the nearest town once a week to sell their produce, but their labourers would hardly see the world outside the village from one Michaelmas to the next. They had their church, their tavern and perhaps a shop, and they needed very little else. For the children a visit to the yearly fair ten miles away was an adventure.

It was in such villages as this, as much as in the towns, that the Baptist cause was born and grew. There were fellowships from the eighteenth century in small Kent communities like Smarden and Headcorn. Eythorne itself, the cradle of the work at Salem, still numbers less than three thousand inhabitants. Almost certainly some of the centres of village worship which were afterwards associated with Salem are in fact older than Salem itself.

No detailed records of the early work around Dover have survived. Letters from the Salem church to the Association mention one 'outstation' from 1843 and two from 1846, and it is likely that one of these was the church at Temple Ewell, where work had been started some years earlier by the church at Eythorne, but in the early Salem minutes there is no other reference to them. They were probably more or less independent fellowships, meeting in a cottage or barn, organising themselves and only needing visits from the larger churches' preachers to supplement the lay workers of their own congregations.

Chapter 5

By the late eighteen sixties, when Salem was preoccupied with its own troubles, it could have been providing very little help for the village congregations. Eythorne, who were obviously still keeping an eye on the fellowship at Temple Ewell, recorded in 1867 that the chapel had been closed for two years. They sold the meeting-house they had been using to the Primitive Methodists in 1871, and used the proceeds to build a more urgently needed place of worship at Ashley. That the fellowship did not fail altogether was due in a large measure to the work of a local lady named Caroline Fector, spinster daughter of a well-known Dover family, who took an interest in the Baptist cause and provided money and encouragement and a place for them to meet in the building which is the present chapel, just across the road from their original venue.

By the late seventies, however, Elijah Edwards had taken charge at Salem and the church, growing and thriving, began to look beyond its own boundaries and take a missionary interest in the villages. In the winter of 1878-9 a series of evangelistic meetings was held, and the work began to revive.

It was a great joy to the church at Salem to see people beginning to gather for worship. But then they needed somewhere to meet. In Temple Ewell, of course, there was no great problem, and in 1883 Caroline Fector not only gave the building where they were meeting and its furniture to them outright, but made over the interest on £750-worth of stock for its upkeep – only stipulating that a Particular Baptist doctrine, 'as taught by C. H. Spurgeon', should always be preached there. In Ewell Minnis there was a little wooden chapel that belonged to the Wesleyan Methodists, and they were willing to allow the Baptists to use it for a nominal rent of one shilling per year. These two congregations thrived in their little chapels. They had no resident pastor, but depended on their own leaders, the general oversight of Salem's minister and the faithful work of a band of local preachers who went out on Sundays to take the services. Special services were held again in the years following and particularly at Temple Ewell the work flourished.

The congregation at St Margaret's were less fortunate. This may also have been a long-established fellowship, but there is no definite information before the1870s. Here too people responded to the evangelistic services, but the group that formed did not find it easy to survive. No-one here offered a building for their use, and worship was not easy in their 'present imperfect acommodation'. Church and chapel were not above vying with one another to attract worshippers, and the Anglicans had the advantage of better buildings and a deeper purse. The situation worried Salem for a number of years. However, in 1887 an idea was born. Perhaps some of their problems might be solved by having a pastor to live and work in the village. Neither the village congregation nor Salem could afford to support a full-time minister there, but perhaps they could contribute to the cost of a colporteur to live at St Margaret's and work in the surrounding area.

The Metropolitan Tabernacle Colportage Association was one of the many enterprises begun by C. H. Spurgeon. Its workers lived in small towns and villages and went round to the houses in the neighbourhood selling religious books and tracts, chatting to people and preaching an informal gospel. They were not ordained men, but as they did this they were also available to lead and encourage the little village churches. They were paid a basic wage partly by the society, which was supported by charitable donations, and partly by a local sponsor. Miss Caroline Fector had provided a colporteur in Temple Ewell for several years before Salem took over, and now the KSBA agreed to place a man in St Margaret's, provided Salem contributed towards his support. In 1889 a man called L.W. Reed was duly appointed, and the situation stabilised.

At first the work moved slowly. They were meeting in a cottage in what is now Chapel Lane, and the spirit of the group improved, but not the numbers. Several people from the village began to come into Dover and worship at Salem; they were evidently the better-off members of the village who could affort transport, and perhaps they found the teaching of Elijah Edwards at Salem more satisfying than that of the colporteur at the chapel. However, in 1894 Reed left and a second man, R. B. Slater, was appointed. He seems to have been an asset to the community. Congregations grew, and in 1898 the Association agreed that its involvement would stretch so far as to put the proceeds from the sale of Dover Tabernacle in Priory Road, which had closed a year or two earlier, towards a proper chapel in the village.

From here the work went from strength to strength. The chapel was opened in 1900, although the burden of paying off the debt lay with Salem and they were not finally rid of it until 1917. Slater continued with them until 1907. He worked hard both at the chapel and at his sales, and some appreciative friends at Salem provided him with a pony and cart for his travels. It was a measure of his popularity in the area – and of the acceptance of the Baptists in general – that at his farewell meeting he was given not only a gift of eight pounds fourteen shillings from the chapel congregation but ten guineas subscribed by the people of the village and handed over by the vicar.

Meanwhile at Salem, Elijah Edwards had been succeeded by Walter Holyoak. The chapels at the other two villages were making progress, though little Ewell Minnis always depended heavily on support from outside. Nevertheless in 1912 the Methodists handed over outright the chapel building there and in 1923 the land on which it stood was made over to Salem as well. At some point the wooden building was replaced by a more substantial meeting room. A Sunday School was begun. During the first world war the services lapsed, but began again in 1920. They started to hold communion services, and in 1925 they held their first communicants' conference.

At Temple Ewell attendance and enthusiasm were variable. In 1914 the church decided to try the idea of a resident pastor there too, and a man named Henry Dobson was appointed and stayed for seven years. The work steadied. A Sunday School had been started many years before, and under Walter Holyoak's guidance it was reorganised and a 'proper system of class teaching' begun. This seems to have had excellent results, so that by the time Dobson left the school was outgrowing the buildings. Howard Bradley and his wife were appointed Superintendents in 1921, and they had been there only two years when the church opened a new 'institute' at the back of the chapel for the use of the Sunday School on Sundays and other groups that met during the week.

So for the two decades between the wars the work at the three chapels prospered. The connection with the Colportage Association was broken in 1909 and by 1932 all three chapels had superintendents from among Salem's

Salem's Associated Chapels

The ladies of the women's meetings at Ewell Minnis (left) and St Margaret's (below) between the wars [photo R. Thomas]

congregation. They improved and extended their buildings, repaired roofs and installed electric light. The Sunday Schools flourished, and women's meetings, sewing circles, and young people's groups were formed.

Sunday services were held in the morning and evening at St Margaret's and Temple Ewell and in the afternoon at Ewell Minnis. Only on special occasions – harvest, anniversary or missionary Sunday – did they enjoy a visit from an ordained minister. On ordinary Sundays the services were taken by a local preacher. These were mostly Salem members, though some came in from Folkestone and Deal. They were not just casual volunteers. From 1931 they were accredited by the Baptist Union, had special training sessions and spent a period as probationers and auxiliaries before they were formally recognised. Few of them would have had transport, except perhaps a bicycle, and it must have been a labour of love for them to travel the three miles out and three miles back once a month or more to minister in a draughty chapel to a congregation of perhaps no more than two dozen. Some of them carried on this service for fifteen or twenty years, and without them the chapels would probably never have survived.

In 1929, with the three chapels well established and flourishing, Salem reached out further and started a new work on the other side of Dover at Capel-le-Ferne. Services were held for a while in the Post Office in the village lent by Mr and Mrs Adams, but a chapel was built in a remarkably short time and was opened on Wednesday 9th July 1930. The opening was a memorable occasion, and not only because of the speakers, the gifts and the renderings from the combined Folkestone and Dover Baptist choirs. As usual the weather in Capel was more extreme than the weather in Dover, and though the actual opening was carried out in sunshine, later in the afternoon while they were holding a service in a marquee a torrential shower fell, rendering the speaker inside almost inaudible and drenching the tables outside laid ready for tea. It is probably as well that the organisers' comments went unrecorded, but they did manage to salvage the food and hastily re-lay the tables inside the marquee for the meal. It is interesting to note that members from Folkestone Baptist Church came to the opening, though their support seems to have stopped there: although Capel is nearer Folkestone than Dover

Salem's Associated Chapels

Salem members on the way to anniversary meetings at Eythorne
[photos J. Fagg, E. Weaver]

Chapter 5

they evidently considered the chapel to be entirely Dover's venture, and apart from the occasional visit of a local preacher there was to be no further input from the Folkestone church for the next thirty years.

So at the beginning of the second world war Salem had four branch chapels. They were part of Salem: if the people came into full membership it was membership of Salem and they were entitled to come to Salem's church meetings, but each chapel had a communicants' conference a few times a year, where those who took communion regularly at the chapel (that is, those who were really committed) had a say in its running. Each had its own Superintendent who oversaw the worship and the meetings and gave pastoral care to the flock. But it could be difficult to find people who would take on that responsibility. Just before the war both St Margaret's and Capel were without leaders. The list of local preachers was declining, too, as the numbers at Salem fell. Then the war began and the villages as well as Dover itself were affected by bombing and evacuation. By the end of the war Leonard Bayly was finding it difficult to cope with the four chapels as well as the main fellowship, and the suggestion of an assistant pastor with special responsibility for the chapels was made, though he left before it was carried out.

Under Islwyn Evans and then under Berkeley Johnson the work rallied a little. Superintendents were found again and were very faithful: between them Jack Connor at Capel, Mark Musk at St Margaret's and David Bradley at Temple Ewell gave almost a hundred years of service. Capel had always had just one meeting on Sundays, and now St Margaret's and Temple Ewell gave up one of their services too so fewer preachers were needed. Berkeley Johnson considered it part of his job to lead worship at the chapels several times a year.

But times had changed. The villages of England were no longer little enclaves of farm workers and the families who served them. Around Dover most of the houses were by now occupied by the retired, those who worked in the tourist industry or commuters from Dover or Folkestone. Fewer people went to church at all, and most of those who did had their own cars and were easily able to travel into the towns on Sundays.

Ewell Minnis was the first to fail. In 1956 the congregation was saddened

Dover (Salem) Baptist Church

Branch Churches Preachers' Plan

1st MAY to 28th AUGUST, 1949

Date 1949	St. Margaret's 10.45 6.30 p.m.	Ewell Minnis 3 p.m.	Temple Ewell 6.30 p.m.	Capel 6.30 p.m.
May 1	* *	Huntley	Fagg	Connor
8	* *	Newport	Sutton	Adams
15	* *	*	Clipsham	Holmes
22	* *	Fagg	Nye	Sutton
29	* *	E.K.L.P.	E.K.L.P.	E.K.L.P.
June 5	* *	Clipsham	Clark	Fagg
12	* *	Clipsham	Huntley	Pierce
19	* *	Walker	Sutton	Clark
26	* *	*	Drinkwater	
July 3	* *	Clipsham	Fagg	Connor
10	* *	Newland	Lipton	Rev. Evans
17	* *	*	Sutton	Huntley
24	* *	Walker	Holmes	Lipton
31	* *	*	Huntley	Fagg
Aug. 7	* *	Clipsham	Robinson	Sutton
14	* *	Fagg	Clipsham	Newport
21	* *	*	Newport	Robinson
28	* *	Newland	Abbott	Huntley

* *Supply to be arranged by Hon. Supt.*

Communion Service—First Sunday of each Month

HYMN BOOKS—St. Margarets   Revised Baptist Church Hymnal
Ewell Minnis   Sankey's "1200"
Temple Ewell   Sankey's "1200"
Capel   Baptist Church Hymnal (1900 Edn.)

Brethren are requested, if unable to fulfil an appointment, to find an acceptable substitute, or communicate with the Superintendent of the mission concerned.

CENTRAL PRESS, 19B HIGH STREET, DOVER

Local preachers' rota 1949

Chapter 5

by the unexpected death at twenty-eight of their young Superintendent, Peter Grant, and after that the work slid steadily down. The gypsies who had camped on the common and had sometimes come to the services disappeared, and the Sunday School declined until unless the leaders took their own children there might be only three or four present. By 1958 there were so few at services that only one local preacher was willing to go out to lead them. They cut the services to one a month. Efforts were made to visit and encourage the local people, but despite some small flickers of life eventually in 1966 the church decided that it simply was not worth trying to continue. The work was closed down and the building was sold.

The other three continued fairly steadily for another twenty years, but congregations were growing smaller. One after another the Sunday Schools closed. The faithful little groups of women continued to meet, listening to equally faithful speakers who were willing to come and talk to groups of ten or a dozen, and there were just enough attending on Sundays to make services worth while. There were flashes of enthusiasm and encouragement. Capel invited Salem to a harvest supper. A Girls' Brigade company was started and run for some years at St Margaret's. A garden party was held there annually – with strong support from Salem – to raise money for the BMS. But overall there was not the interest among the village people themselves, and the other three chapels were in danger of expiring.

At last, in 1982, a church meeting was held at Salem, under the moderator Clifford Gill, and the situation was put before the members. It was not enough to keep the chapels ticking over: they must change or die. After prayerful consideration the church decided to take positive steps.

St Margaret's would close down altogether. Those Salem members who were concerned for the work there would put their efforts into a youth club run by the Anglicans. Only one of the people who still worshipped at the chapel on Sundays was a Salem member, and she was willing to be brought into Dover by car. The other three regular attenders would be happy to attend the Anglican church in the village. Services would cease and the building would be sold.

Capel was to be taken over by the church at Rendezvous Street, Folkestone.

Capel Chapel exterior 1970s

There had been a suggestion from there in 1962 that the chapel might share the ministry of a deaconess with their own daughter church, Hill Road Baptist, but at that time Salem did not feel they could afford the £75 per year Folkestone were asking as a contribution to her salary. But now Salem, realising that the alternative was to close it, suggested to Folkestone that they might take Capel chapel over entirely, and after a year's trial they agreed.

This left Temple Ewell. Two Salem couples came forward offering to take over the leadership at Temple Ewell, and several other families who lived in the River and Temple Ewell area were willing to leave Salem entirely and go out to give all their support in the village. It would leave a gap in the fellowship at Salem, but it offered a new impetus at the chapel and gave hope that it still might one day become an independent cause. These couples, Liz and Alan

Chapter 5

Hibell and Pat and Arthur Clipsham, would not be called Superintendents, but together with Derek Donne the treasurer, who already worshipped there regularly, would become a 'leadership team'. They were commissioned at Salem on 16th June 1991, and were given £2000 to allow the work a fresh start.

So for the last years of the century the work in the villages began to move forward again. At St Margaret's the youth club was started, after a year or two became a Covenanters group, and continued so through the rest of the century. Services at the parish church were evangelical and some Baptists from the village were happy to join them. Others found it quite possible to come by car every week to Salem. The chapel was put up for sale, and though it proved difficult to find a buyer, mainly because there was no vehicle access from the road, it was eventually sold to the St Margaret's Bay Trust and used as a meeting place for various village activities.

At Capel the people of Folkestone Baptist (now at Hill Road) have continued the work faithfully under Clifford Gill, Ewen Blaker and now Alan Smith. The building has had new windows and a new kitchen put in, and the fellowship meets for prayer and Bible study and for a craft group, a coffee drop-in and regular meals together as well as worship on Sundays. Numbers from the village are still small, but the work is well supported by the Folkestone church members, and there is a spirit of warmth and encouragement that promises well for the future.

At Temple Ewell the team spent several years thoroughly renovating and re-decorating the chapel to make it more attractive to worshippers. A Bible Study group was started, and the single afternoon service was changed to a morning service and an evening 'prayer and share' meeting. A mission was held and efforts were made to reach the villagers. Then they started a children's club, and the children from the village primary school not only came enthusiastically on Friday afternoons but brought their parents to special services on Sundays as well. In 1999 Liz and Alan Hibell decided that their place should after all be at Salem and returned there. But the Spirit continues to move at Temple Ewell. There is an average Sunday attendance of twenty-five, and between 1991 and 2001 six people have been baptised and come

Salem's Associated Chapels

The opening of the Temple Ewell institute in 1926 [photo courtesy of Dover Express

The 'institute' in use on the chapel's anniversary in 1993 [photo D. Oram]

CHAPTER 5

into membership.

So at the beginning of the new century, of the four chapels which were once under Salem's care only Temple Ewell remains. The work in all the villages has been worthwhile; no-one can say how many people have been influenced by the witness of the men and women who served there. In Capel and St Margaret's that work has not ceased; it goes forward, though in other forms. But only Temple Ewell remains attached to Salem.

There has been a change of outlook in the past decade, and now the Temple Ewell church is considered not so much a dependant as a partner, a smaller fellowship but equal in accountability and having an equal share of the time and work of the minister. In 2000 the church adopted the logo that was designed for Temple Ewell in 1992. And underneath the words were added, 'Two fellowships, one church'.

70th anniversary cake at Capel in 2000 [photo Alison Smith]

Chapter 6
Youth

For the church at Salem, as for many other organisations, children have always been both a bane and a blessing. The church is a family and includes young and old, but the old sometimes feel that the church would be a more civilised place without the young. Young people fidget during the services and ask questions afterwards. They have too much energy: they risk their necks jumping off the stage or sliding down the bannisters (the stairs from the gallery at old Salem were particularly good for this); they kick balls through windows or against the burglar alarm sensor; they make a noise that irritates their elders, and rush about and get in the way of the less agile. This has always been so, and those who think that children were better behaved in their young days are voicing a sentiment that was old before Salem was built.

But this energy is a spring of new life, and without it the church would grow stale and dull before it was altogether extinguished. It needs directing, but it is vital – and it is worth noticing that some of the naughtiest boys (Roy Connor and Maurice Chandler among them) grew into some of the strongest and most useful men of the new generation. The church at Salem has always made provision for the young people, and has done its best to teach and train them and to direct all that energy into useful channels.

There is a tradition that the Salem Sunday School began even before the church. A banner made in 1885 bore the words 'formed in 1838', though there is no other evidence for this date. What is definitely recorded is that on the first Sunday that the church met for worship in Military Road the Sunday School met too, with 'about twenty-four children'. It seems to have flourished, rising to sixty children the next year and ninety by 1843.

Chapter 6

At this time Sunday Schools were quite different from Sunday Schools today. They had been begun about fifty years earlier for the poorest children of the industrial towns, with the dual intention of keeping them off the streets on Sundays and of teaching them to read. Salem's Sunday School would have been of this kind, teaching the alphabet first and then using simple primers and eventually ensuring that the children could read the Bible before they left at about twelve or thirteen. A certain amount of moral and spiritual teaching would have been inevitable, given the content of the books they used, but the primary goal was simply to enable them to read the Bible for themselves. For reasons which are difficult to follow today, in many schools – Salem obviously among them – reading was acceptable but writing was seen as 'work' and so not allowed on the Sabbath. Accordingly in 1843 Mrs E.B. Hewlett offered to start a class to teach the older girls to read on a weeknight, an offer which was gladly accepted.

The school grew as the church grew. In 1845 a Sunday School library was started (with £5 from the church funds and two gifts of books from the Religious Tract Society), so that, in those days before public libraries, the children had access to books to read. When the church went through difficulties in the 1860s the number of scholars fell, but once Elijah Edwards had taken the reins it went on from strength to strength. Before the building was enlarged in 1880 there was hardly space for all those who came, and even in the new rooms four hundred children and thirty-nine teachers must have sat crammed together, and much movement would have been out of the question. In these circumstances infection could spread with ease, and in 1893 the mayor asked for the Sunday School to be closed for several Sundays because of the illness among the children of the town. Boys and girls were separated, the boys at the front of the building and the girls at the back. The infants had their own room where they sat in tiers on a kind of wooden scaffolding. By now the teaching of reading had passed largely into the hands of the day schools, and Sunday Schools were concentrating on spiritual teaching. This must have seemed the more urgent because there was a real possibility that some of the children who attended would die before they reached adulthood, and the teachers would have been aware that their salvation

> ❛May 1885. The Sub-committee . . . having recommended that a new banner for the school be procured, it was resolved that the banner be 6 $^1/_2$ feet by 5 including fringe and that it be made of dark blue silk with golden letters. That the text Glory to God in the highest with Salem Sunday School 1838 be inscribed thereon, and that an estimate be obtained through Mr J Flashman.
>
> Sept 1885. The treasurer . . . reported that the new banner, which cost £11.19, was paid for.❜
>
> *(Sunday School Teachers Meeting minutes)*

might depend on their hearing and understanding the gospel at Salem on a Sunday.

By now virtually every church and chapel in the country had its Sunday School, and the National Sunday School Union worked very hard for their help and encouragement. In 1880 Sunday Schools all over the country held events to celebrate the centenary of their founding. In Dover one June afternoon more than five thousand children, representing twenty-six schools, formed up in Pencester Road and marched up to the fields by the castle. There they had games and tea (one buttered huffkin, one jammed huffkin, a slice of cake and a quart of milk-and-water each) and were given a toy and a centenary mug before they marched back again. All this was paid for by the mayor, Richard Dickeson, who though an Anglican himself included all the churches of the town in his generosity.

This was the heyday of Sunday Schools. At the end of the century more than eighty per cent of the country's five to fourteen-year-olds attended Sunday Schools, and there were over five hundred children at Salem. But attitudes to church-going were changing, and slowly the numbers at Salem, as elsewhere, began to creep down again. By the nineteen thirties they had fallen below three hundred. The members of that time looked back with regret to past glories, though for us, looking back in our turn, three hundred seems glory enough. Out of a church membership of nearly three hundred and fifty it was

Chapter 6

Sunday School treat at Old Park about 1912

fairly easy to find more than thirty teachers for them (which is very much the same proportion of teachers to the overall membership as we have today).

Once the new block was opened in 1910 there was scope for more adventurous teaching. The school still met together at the beginning of the session, boys on one side of the hall and girls on the other, but then they separated to the various rooms to be taught in smaller groups. Movement was possible: in 1920 the infants were marching round their room singing 'Hear the pennies dropping' before they dropped the said pennies into a box in the middle. More space, though, did not necessarily mean better teaching. Telling stories to infants seemed such a simple thing that teachers did not always see the need for training or preparation. For many years the National Sunday School Union had been trying to persuade teachers to use lesson 'helps' and attend preparation classes, and in 1928 it is recorded that the KSBA was echoing them; classes were begun at Salem but for many years after that there are pleas that all the teachers should actually attend them. But there were teachers who taught, and no doubt taught well, for many years, considering this their service to God. Several Salem teachers (Mr Foord and Mr Crepin, for instance, in 1919) were awarded the NSSU's long service diploma for teaching for over twenty-five years.

It was not always easy. The teachers found that if they tried to include children from the poorest and roughest homes in the town they simply disrupted the lessons, and yet these needed the gospel as much as Salem's own children. In 1921 the church decided to begin a separate service for these 'untrained' children and a weeknight meeting 'of a varied nature'. How long this continued before it was amalgamated with the normal classes is not recorded. After the second world war, by which time the Pier district had been demolished but the new Buckland estate was full of young families with children, a special bus service was arranged with the East Kent Road Car company, to bring forty or fifty children down each week to Sunday School at Salem.

The Sunday School year was punctuated by special events. In the summer they had an outing to Old Park or Kearsney where they played games and ran races. At Christmas there was a party. The Sunday School anniversary could be quite an occasion: in 1921 they had services on Sunday and Monday, a 'workers' conference' on Tuesday, a children's evening on Wednesday and a thanksgiving on Thursday. The Sunday School anniversary was celebrated separately from the church anniversary, with special songs and dramatic presentations by the children, until 1962.

Gradually, as the twentieth century passed, sending children to Sunday School became the exception rather than the rule. Salem's numbers dwindled, and it became more difficult to find people to teach, especially, it is noted, on the boys' side. For many years the Salem Sunday School had met in the afternoon, though at various periods there had been a morning school as well. But by mid-century families were going out in their cars or visiting their families on Sunday afternoons, and in 1964 the afternoon school was abandoned. The new morning school took the form which is still followed, with occasional exceptions, today: the children come into church for the first part of the morning service and then leave for thirty to forty minutes of lessons on their own. The lessons were changing as well. The core of Bible

CHAPTER 6

teaching remained, but by now the representations of the educators were being heeded, and it was presented through craft, drama, and games. This was partly from a genuine effort to make the teaching memorable and relevant to the children, but partly from concern that without such an interesting format the children would not stay. Bored children very soon vote with their feet, and parents who were neutral, or perhaps not altogether sorry to be able to have a lie-in on Sunday mornings, would be unlikely to insist. It became necessary as it had not been a hundred years before to entice the children in and woo them to stay.

Over a century and a half, not all the work with young people, any more than all the work with adults, has been concentrated on Sundays. When Salem was built the church's work concentrated almost entirely on the care of souls. People were reached by straightforward preaching, in sermon, tract or mission, and worship and Bible study were presented as a discipline. But as the century passed strategies changed. Children as well as adults began to be encouraged to join in activities on the fringe of the church in the hope that

Salem young people's choir about 1957, with Islwyn Evans, middle row centre, and Oliver Hoskin, choirmaster, front row centre.

> 'The Pastor reported the bequest to the church of a piano by the late Mrs Martin, who requested that it should not be used in the Schoolroom used by the Boys.' *Church Minutes October 1921*

there they would feel at home in the church family, and would begin to recognise their spiritual emptiness and come further in and meet with their Saviour.

The young people's societies were at first basically religious, though no doubt when the youngsters met on a weeknight they contrived to gain a fair amount of social enjoyment as well. There were Bible Classes for boys and for girls, and a Christian Band, where new young Christians received solid Bible teaching. The Young People's Christian Endeavour society was formed at Salem in 1898, and re-formed after the war in 1919. This was a branch of the national Christian Endeavour Union, a society begun to encourage young people at the top end of the Sunday School to gather on a week-night for study and discussion on Christian themes. The Salem leaders did not keep too strictly to the set national programme, though: as someone said in 1919, 'he thought it would attract young men to the weekly meeting if it had more up-to-date present day topics, and he did not think a programme with old testament prophets and stories tended to promote interest in the Society among young non-members', a comment which might have been made any time in the past two hundred – indeed two thousand – years. They decided to alter the topics or the titles where necessary to make them more appealing, and they held lantern lectures and testimony evenings and question times, and in the summer garden meetings or rambles. It sounds attractive, and seems to have flourished.

The Band of Hope was another young people's meeting that ran for about forty years around the turn of the century. The people of Salem, like most nonconformist churches at that time, were strongly involved in the temperance movement, and by the end of the century this was concentrating most of its efforts on catching and teaching the young. The Band of Hope was always closely allied with Sunday School work, and the meetings were well attended.

Chapter 6

How many of the young people who came really understood the underlying issues or made an informed decision about alcohol it is impossible to say, but between 1879 and 1888 it is recorded that six hundred and seventy-eight young people had 'taken the pledge'. Certainly a whole generation of Salem people was firmly, even vehemently, teetotal.

The Christian Endeavour and Band of Hope meetings were on the whole sedentary affairs with speakers and songs and discussions. Rather wider-ranging in their activities were the uniformed organisations that began about the same time. The Boys Brigade was a national organisation founded in 1883 by William Smith. It was intended to attract teenage boys to the church by offering week-night meetings with army-style drill and exercise, and camping in the summer. For those churches who disliked the idea of military training in a Christian organisation the Boys Life Brigade was begun in 1899, run on similar lines but without the drill and offering swimming and life-saving as its main attraction. A Boys Life Brigade company was started at Salem in 1907, and it must have seemed to its officers a justification of all they had taught when they were able to offer boys trained in first aid to help the war effort in 1914. The company seems itself to have been a casualty of the war, though, and took some years to re-form afterwards. In 1926 the BLB and BB amalgamated nationally, and a BB company was formed at Salem in 1938 only to close again almost at once. After the war it seems to have been difficult to find officers, perhaps partly because the young men of the right age were going off at that period to do their National Service. It was eventually re-started in 1957, but it only lasted about ten years more before closing altogether.

The Girls' Life Brigade (founded nationally in 1902) ran more steadily and for longer at Salem. The company began in 1913. It too had to be closed down during the first world war, but it began again in 1919 and continued until the second. It was started up again in 1948 and then ran without a break (only with a change of name when three organisations amalgamated in 1965 to become The Girls Brigade) until 1987. Like the boys, the girls marched, drilled and wore uniform, though probably the girls on the whole found this less satisfying than the boys. There was also a variety of other tests and badges, and (unlike the otherwise similar Guides) each company had to be attached

YOUTH

Boys Brigade early 1960s [photo J. Cook]

Girls Brigade, South East Kent district 1968 [photo Ray Warner]

Chapter 6

to a church and there was a strong spiritual dimension. The links with the national organisation were strong, and the Salem girls competed with other local companies, attended combined church parades and visited the Albert Hall for the annual national rally. For many years girls and officers went off for a week during the summer to camp in church halls in a variety of seaside locations.

Most of the organisations that began before the war were affiliated to a country-wide network, and most were basically educational. It was not till the nineteen forties that throughout the country a fashion began for social activities for young people. Just before the war a social club was formed at Salem and, in 1945 it became the Youth Fellowship. This was not connected with any wider group, and there was no compulsion to follow any set programme. The group could be allowed to plan its own meetings and organise whatever activities it wanted, although it was always understood that meetings should include some devotional time. The young people could play table tennis and billiards, arrange outings or drama or simply come to sit and chat. This was both an advantage and a disadvantage. It meant freedom to do what appealed to the particular interests of the members, but it also meant that the club depended heavily on the quality of its leadership. In Islwyn Evans' time, with his interest in and gift for reaching young people, the YPF met twice a week, and a young people's choir and badminton club grew up as well. Later on, there were sometimes concerns about how the club was organised and the kinds of activities that took place there. It is clear that though it continued in one form or another until the nineteen eighties its size and effectiveness fluctuated greatly over the years.

In the first half of the twentieth century church-based clubs and organisations had accounted for many of the leisure activities available to young people. Gradually from the nineteen sixties things changed. Church-based groups began to be seen as authoritarian and narrow-minded. The standard of living was going up and parents were prepared to pay for specialised equipment and qualified instruction, so that clubs and societies grew up with no church connections - sports clubs, music groups, drama societies. At the same time, church membership was falling and there were not so many people available to undertake the work of the church, so youth leaders were not so easily found. At Salem, gradually, one by one, the youth groups closed. The Band of Hope and Covenanters were long gone, but in 1969 the Boys' Brigade and in 1987 the Girls' Brigade had to close for lack of officers. The youth clubs took over for a while. In 1985 there were three youth clubs for different age-groups, but between then and 1991 their leaders gradually left the church or left Dover or took on other jobs, and one after another the clubs closed. Only the Sunday School kept going, but since one of the functions of the week-night groups had been to attract children into the church their closing meant that by the end of the twentieth century there were few children in the Sunday School who did not belong to church families.

However, the picture is not all gloomy. Though the Sunday School (re-named Sunday Workshop in 1984) is small, it is healthy. The children are regular and enthusiastic. Recently there has been an effort to integrate the children more closely with the rest of the congregation, and to that end birthdays are celebrated during the service, young people lead prayers and songs from time to time, and the children now attend the communion service. Although there are now no weekly evening meetings several holiday clubs have been organised over the past two decades, and a small number of adults has been willing to organise occasional social activities for teenagers. In 2000 a youth leader was once more appointed, and it is hoped that in the next few years the youth work will be able to expand again.

Salem is not alone in having difficulty in finding children's workers, and it has been encouraging in the last decade to see members of several Dover churches coming together to share the load. Spring Kids was begun in 1992, arising out of the combined churches' Tell Dover mission; it has leaders from churches including Baptists, Anglicans, Catholics and Apostolics, and holds two or three meetings each year for five to eleven-year-olds from any of the churches and schools in the area. Out of this grew SKY (Spring Kids Youth) for eleven to fourteens, and then a fourteen-plus group, who have converted the crypt at Charlton (C of E) Church for use as a drop-in centre for young people on Friday nights.

Children's work at Salem has varied enormously over the life-span of the

Chapter 6

Spring Kids holiday club at Salem 1990s. [photo D. Oram]

Sunday Workshop children dressed for the Christmas play 2000 [photo J. Booth]

Members of Sunday Workshop handing over 'Love in a Box' gifts to a representative from Mustard Seed Relief Missions, for children in Eastern Europe. Christmas 2000. [photo D. Oram]

church. It began with a single Sunday School, widened into a range of different meetings and activities at the beginning of the twentieth century, and then slowly fell back to a single Sunday School again. But it has not ceased. Circumstances have changed, but the church is still concerned for its children – as it needs to be. They are not just a valuable part of the church of today. They are the church of the future.

> **'** There is a tendency, not only in our own day, but in past generations, even to Old Testament days, to deprecate the younger generation, but let us remember that a church without young people is a dying church.**'** *(F. A. Holmes, secretary's report 1952)*

CHAPTER 7
Loving our neighbours

THE two great commandments linked together by Jesus were to love God and to love your neighbour. It is obvious that the first is a central principle for the church; it is the primary reason for its existence. The second is just as important, but Christians have not always found it easy to decide how far that love should concentrate on saving their neighbour's soul and how far it should help to feed and clothe his body. They have had to try to follow the example of the man who healed the sick and fed the hungry, and yet thought material comfort and security of so little importance that he lived homeless and died as a criminal, and expected his followers to be willing to do the same.

But whenever the church has been strong, caring for the poor and disadvantaged has been an important part of its life. Certainly over the years of Salem's existence the members have cared for each other, and in many instances they have cared for the welfare of those outside as well.

It seems likely, though there is no specific record, that there were funds kept available to help the poor from the very beginning; it was certainly so by the eighteen seventies. For very many years an offering was taken at the communion service and used for this purpose, sometimes supplemented by extra gifts from members. Generally speaking the money has been at the disposal of the minister, so that he can give it to people in need without having to account to the church for specific gifts. This has on one or two occasions led to friction when the money seems to have been distributed unwisely or no records kept, but mostly the church has been happy to trust to his judgement. The money was generally used for the church's own poor but the connection did not have to be close: in 1889 a former member who had moved away died in Eastbourne, leaving a widow and a large family of young children, and that month's communion offering was made up from the communion fund to £7 10s (more than a month's wages) and sent to her with Christian greetings.

Giving money is simple and direct. The disadvantage, however, is that the giver has no control how the money will be spent, and those who are careful with their money can understandably be reluctant to give it away to those who they suspect are in difficulties precisely because they have not been careful. This is perhaps one reason why the church has tended to offer help in kind rather than in cash; another reason is that there is more personal contact in making a cup of tea than in handing over a shilling.

The winter of 1885–6 was a bad one. In Dover, as in many other parts of the country, there was deep snow for weeks, and widespread unemployment. There was virtually no state relief then for the able-bodied and the wages most of the men earned even in good times would not carry them over a long period out of work. The Mayor of Dover, W.J. Adcock, had set up a fund during the winter to pay some of the neediest to work on making a public garden along the path from old St James' church up to the Castle, and Salem contributed willingly to this, but they felt that something more was required, so they also organised a free tea at the chapel for sixty of the men and their wives. It would be interesting to know how much they talked to the participants as they served the meal. They followed the tea with an evangelistic service; whether the men concerned felt that the tea was worth the preaching is not told, but it was during that same year that sixty-eight people were baptised, so it could be that some of those who came to get food for their bodies also received food for their souls.

Again in 1927, in the aftermath of the General Strike, free dinners and teas were given to the children of the unemployed. Nor has the need to feed the poor vanished with the coming of the welfare state. In many areas nowadays it is difficult for voluntary organisations to compete with professionals, but one way in which ordinary church members in Dover can be involved with the less fortunate is at the 'soup run', brought into being in 1991 by Stephanie Perrow of River Methodist Church. There are still those who for varying

Chapter 7

reasons are without money, and the soup run offers soup and sandwiches without charge at six o'clock each evening to anyone who comes to a cabin in one of the town's car parks. It is run on a rota basis by about eight of the churches of the town. Those who come - on average around a dozen - are often sleeping rough or moving about in search of work. Few of them appear totally destitute and from time to time the providers ask themselves how genuine the need is, but most of them are noticeably grateful for what is offered.

But mostly the provision of food has been a means of making social contact. Often those who come to eat or drink are those within the church or congregation. 'Tea meetings' go back to the very early days at Salem, when drinking tea together was combined with a business meeting or a fund-raising event. A century and a half later the church is still gathering to eat together socially. We have Christmas dinners and Easter breakfasts, we eat after the morning service or before the evening service, we hold barbecues in the summer and coffee mornings at all seasons.

Barbecue at River

LOVING OUR NEIGHBOURS

Christmas dinner at Salem

The Women's Fellowship Christmas dinner cooks

Chapter 7

But frequently the contact has been with people outside the church. Between November 1914 and October 1918 Salem provided over eleven thousand teas for servicemen, some of the cost being covered by a grant from the military authorities and some by Salem people themselves. When tighter rationing at the end of the war made the provision of full-scale teas impossible they continued the Social Hour with 'light refreshments' until the middle of 1919. In the second world war two rooms were made available all day to the men, with volunteers selling refreshments at minimum prices. It was hardly home from home, but there were queues each day waiting for the rooms to open, so at least for some of the time and for some of the men it must have been a welcome alternative to the pub.

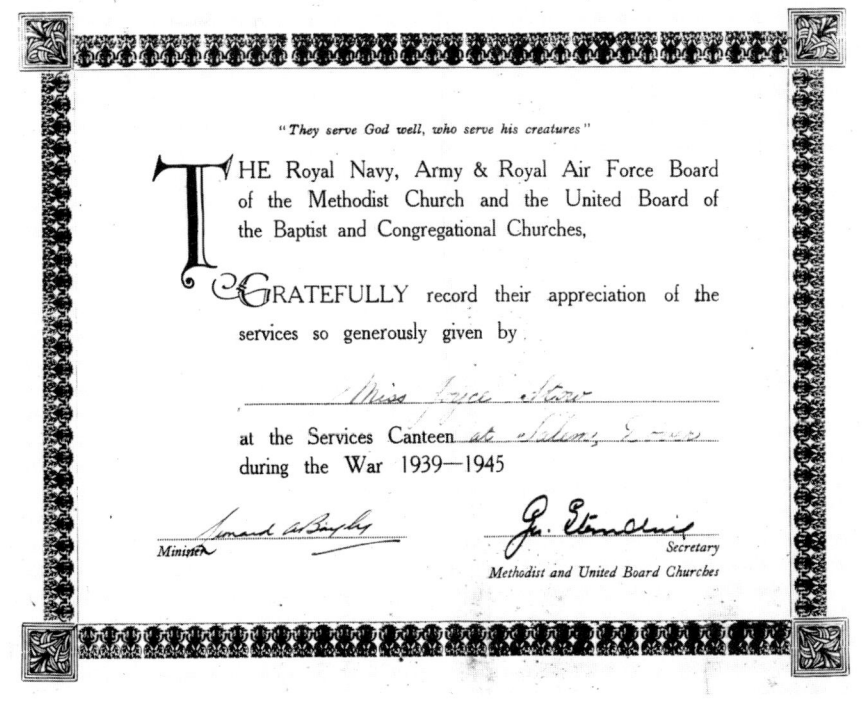

"They serve God well, who serve his creatures"

THE Royal Navy, Army & Royal Air Force Board of the Methodist Church and the United Board of the Baptist and Congregational Churches,

GRATEFULLY record their appreciation of the services so generously given by

Miss Joyce Stow

at the Services Canteen at Salem, ...

during the War 1939—1945

Minister

Secretary
Methodist and United Board Churches

Certificate given to Joyce Stow (now Joyce Fagg) for helping in the Salem canteen for servicemen 1939–45

For about thirty years in the mid-twentieth century a Luncheon Club flourished, when volunteers cooked a two-course meal at Salem every Tuesday for fifty people or more, and at the moment a similar scheme on a smaller scale offers a light meal between two meetings on Wednesday lunch-time. Both these have made a modest charge, but those who have taken advantage of them – many of them people who live alone – are glad to be free of the cooking and to enjoy company at the table; the need being met here is not money but friendship.

There have been other ways of meeting material need, too. For half a century from 1873 a group of Salem women ran a Dorcas Society. The name comes from the story of Dorcas in Acts chapter 9, and the intention presumably was that ladies with time to spare met together to make clothes for the poor. It is not known how the poor received these gifts. Early in the society's life they are seen making winter clothes for the girls of 'Dr Barnardo's institution', but by the nineteen thirties the society had outlived its original purpose and had turned to making articles for sale to help church funds. Another, perhaps more imaginative enterprise was the church's maternity box. This was in existence for about ten years at the beginning of the twentieth century, and was made available to women whose confinements put a strain on an already tight budget. It held bed-linen, night-clothes and baby-clothes (and a Bible) and could be borrowed by respectable women (applicants must be married and be recommended by two ladies of the church) in strict order of application. Half a crown was also given to the mother towards other expenses. The clothes were supposed to be returned clean, though once or twice it is noted that someone had to be paid to wash them before they went out again.

Practical help of other kinds has been offered from time to time. Several times during the twentieth century a group has been organised for the mothers of pre-school children: a Young Wives and Mothers' meeting in 1952, a kindergarten in 1966, and a Mums and Toddlers group in 1980. All had a moderate success. In 1985 two ladies who had experience with the multitudinous form-filling of modern society offered their assistance one morning a week to the unemployed, or anyone else who came to seek it. The response was small but appreciative.

Chapter 7

All these enterprises have been attempts by Salem people to help those on their doorstep. At the end of the nineteenth century they also became involved with a much wider-scale activity, the temperance movement. Dover had its share of drunkenness. In the middle of the century there had been one pub in the town for every hundred inhabitants (and that figure includes women and children). Historians nowadays disagree whether the abject poverty of some of the working class at that time was really caused by drink, or whether on the contrary it was the poverty that led to the drinking. But to the non-conformist churches of the day there was no doubt about it and for some fifty years they made strenuous efforts to divert the money back from the pub to the family and to provide an alternative lifestyle for the working man. Elijah Edwards and Walter Holyoak were both staunch supporters of the movement. They were involved with the town's Temperance Council and encouraged the organisation of Salem's own Total Abstinence Society, which was formed in 1892 and ran till 1913. They held regular meetings at Salem and supported Temperance Missions and open-air demonstrations. One of the trustees of the new buildings in 1910 was the proprietor of a Temperance Hotel. There was also a Band of Hope, the children's branch, which did its best to persuade children of the evils of drink while they were still young enough to be easily persuaded, and this in fact outlived the adult society.

And in many instances private action is not enough; what is needed is government intervention. The people of Salem have never felt that the church should have no dealings with politics. They wrote to the government urging stricter licensing laws in 1892, 1921 and 1923, and they disapproved of the introduction of a betting tax and the licensing of bookmakers in 1923. They protested against the ill-treatment of natives in the Congo in 1907, against the opium traffic from India to China in 1910, against slavery in parts of the British Empire in 1931, and against the use of napalm weapons in 1952. In 1972 they supported the KSBA who wrote to congratulate Lord Longford on his stand against pornography, and in 1988 the Evangelical Alliance who were protesting against Sunday Trading. At the millennium they added their names to the Jubilee 2000 appeal for the cancellation of the Third World debt. Small though their voice may be, it is the voice of some part of the

Chapter 7

Picnicking on a Church outing

electorate. Those in high places working for debt reduction in 2000 were surprised and encouraged by the strength of the support from the country's churches.

It is impossible, of course, to record all the efforts of the church to reach out to help those around it. Many, perhaps most of those efforts have been private individual acts, not written in any minute book. Salem ministers have been governors or chaplains in the hospital, police force and schools. Members have served as magistrates, worked at the 'Sailors' Refuge', at the Riverside Centre for the elderly, or among the town's youth; others have quietly and without fanfare visited the sick and house-bound, shopped for the incapacitated, taken the blind on holiday, cleaned houses, offered hospitality to the lonely, given lifts to those without transport, written letters or listened patiently to innumerable boring and inconvenient phone-calls. We have taken the call to love our neighbour seriously.

Nonetheless, all these are things which might be – and frequently are –

done by those outside the church as well as those inside. The church's distinctive contribution is not only to care for the material needs of its neighbours but to proclaim the love of God for their souls.

(Left) Visiting the elderly at Allandale about 1994 [photo D. Oram]
(Bottom) Coffee 'n' chat 2000 and the chocolate cake competition [photo J. Booth]

Chapter 8
Mission

IF Christianity is true, then it is true for everyone. If the gospel is good news then it is worth sharing. And if you are convinced, as the early nineteenth century evangelicals were, that anyone who is not trusting in Christ's saving grace is on his way to hell, then you can't look at those outside the church without an urgent desire at least to make them aware of their destination and if possible to save them from it.

Throughout its life the church at Salem has tried to reach those beyond its walls. The Sunday School, which began at the same time as the church itself, taught the children of the neighbourhood and through them had a certain amount of contact with the parents. On Sunday afternoons in the 1840s a large group of the new church was involved in Sunday School work, but of those who were not busy with the children another group went out to visit the houses of the surrounding neighbourhood. Their aim was, they said, to make Christ known to 'the destitute, the sick, the aged', though presumably they were willing to speak to others as well if they showed an interest.

It is very likely that as they visited they gave tracts to the householders they met. Tracts had been around for most of that century. Those taken out to the neighbourhood would have been pamphlets declaiming the Christian message in simple, dramatic form. 'SEE,' proclaimed a very popular one, 'The dreadful gulf is beneath you, A few more steps in the way of sin and headlong down you go into eternal fire . . . ESCAPE! for your life!!!' – before going on to the cross and the way of escape provided. They were as effective as the advertisements they mimicked, and were widely used by the evangelical churches of the day. By 1844 the Salem visitors had been organised into a Tract Distribution Society, which lasted a remarkably long time. People were still regularly delivering tracts almost a century later. By 1936 some members were questioning the value of putting out material that did not bear the name of the church, and by the end of the second world war tract distribution as a regular activity seems to have faded away – though many efforts to reach the neighbourhood over the years have begun with a delivery of flyers of one kind or another, and leaflets setting out the Christian message are still to be found on display in the church entrance-hall for visitors to pick up and read. A church magazine has been distributed, too, beginning in 1926, with several different formats over the years but with much the same intention, to give information about church affairs to members and to catch the interest of those on the fringes of the congregation and in the surrounding neighbourhood.

In the early days the church at Salem seems to have concentrated on steady individual effort at evangelism rather than intensive campaigns. There is mention of a United Town Mission in Dover in 1841, but Salem seems to have been contributing money to it rather than manpower. They were aware, too, of the work of the Baptist Missionary Society working overseas. This had been in existence for some fifty years when Salem was built, but interest generally in England was limited at that time, and it does not appear that this church was any more eager than most in its support. Early references are few. They held a missionary meeting in 1858, just after Alexander Pitt had resigned, but the minutes dismissed it in eight words: 'The chapel was cold, and the attendance small'. It appears that there was no great enthusiasm among the members for the work beyond England's shores.

In 1873, however, things began to change. Captain Passingham was a man informed and enthusiastic about missionary matters. While he was on military service in India he had discovered and admired the work of the BMS there, and when he came home and left the army he spent much time promoting its work in the churches of this country. During his ministry a missionary society was formed at Salem, aiming to raise funds which were to be divided equally between the Baptist Missionary Society for the work overseas and the Baptist Home Missionary Society for work in this country. It was while Passingham was in Redruth on deputation that he first met Elijah Edwards, and it was because he was wondering whether he might go back and make a tour of BMS stations in India that he asked Edwards to consider taking over the ministry in Dover.

The two must have found each other congenial company, for Elijah Edwards was also a man with a heart for mission. One of his brothers, Rev. T. Llewellyn Edwards, was assistant pastor at the Metropolitan Tabernacle where Spurgeon had started such an outreach among the people of London, and another, Dr Ebenezer Edwards, was working with the China Inland Mission. Elijah had no such great mission field to work, but he laboured unceasingly in the place he had. Slowly but thoroughly he began to teach the people of Salem to care not only about the unsaved on their own doorstep, but about those one step beyond Dover and then about those on the other side of the world.

In Dover itself Sunday by Sunday the tract distributors continued their work. The church also began to hold missions to the town. In 1880 they joined with other free churches to hold a series of meetings, most of which took place in various chapels and schoolrooms but one of which was large enough to need the town's skating rink. In 1885 they began to hold weekly evangelistic meetings after the ordinary Sunday evening service, and the next year there was another united mission led by a Mr Henry Varley, where 'the advantage to Christians of all denominations was great and many persons were brought from the world to Christ.' The mission to the local area became an event in the church's life that recurred at intervals for the next seventy years, an intensive effort to reach the outsider that supplemented and reinforced the day-to-day work of the faithful.

In the villages too they began to perceive a harvest field. When Edwards began his ministry any earlier work at Ewell Minnis, Temple Ewell and St Margaret's was at a very low ebb, and for several years the church from Salem went out to hold missions among the villagers. People came, people were converted, and new buildings had to be found to house the expanded congregations. A light was lit there in the 1880s that shone for almost a century.

And then they looked abroad. In the late nineteenth century ever more countries were coming formally under British rule, and pride in the Empire

Chapter 8

> 'We praise God for those who thinking not of themselves, go forth to preach the glorious words of redeeming love.'
>
> *Association letter 1924*

was at its height. For Christians it was a world to be saved. 'How shall they believe in him of whom they have not heard?' they read in Romans, 'And how shall they hear without a preacher?' Under Passingham's influence the people of Salem had begun to hold an annual meeting to raise funds for the BMS, and by the mid-eighteen eighties they were contributing sixty or seventy pounds each year to the work of foreign missions, as well as making occasional collections for famine relief in various places. Now, encouraged by Elijah Edwards, they began to invite men to come and tell them about the work, and listened with increasing interest. In 1889 Ebenezer Edwards, home on furlough, came to talk about the work of the interdenominational China Inland Mission. He 'stirred up greater interest in foreign mission work, especially in that great empire', and as well as the church increasing its already generous giving, more than one of his listeners heard God's call to go out and serve him overseas.

In November 1891 a farewell meeting was held for the first of these, George Stokes. He had grown up in Salem; he had been a teacher in the Sunday School at Salem and at St Margaret's, and now he was leaving for the wider mission field. It was an occasion to be remembered. There were speeches from the staff of the Sunday School and a talk from a member of CIM describing the life he would be going to, and the meeting wished him Godspeed and arranged to give regular contributions to support him in his work. He made the six-week sea journey and arrived in China in January 1892.

He was the first of a tide of men and women who heard the same call. During the next thirty years twelve men and women left Salem for work in foreign fields (as well as four who became ministers in this country or in

George and Margaret Stokes

others), and their letters and their talks when they came home kept the church's missionary interest alive and eager for half a century and more. Their fields of service varied. Some were evangelistic missionaries pure and simple; most carried out other work as well. George Stokes left the China Inland Mission after a few years to work with Dr Edwards and a group of other missionaries in a town called T'ai-Yüan Fu, where there was a Christian bookshop and a hospital as well as a church. Hilda Bradley worked in India as a nurse. George Hicks spent many years overseeing the 'leper asylum' at Ganga, India, and in 1918 he received the Kaiser-i-Hind medal in recognition of his work there.

The life of a missionary at that time was hard. Their call was usually for life; travel was slow for both people and mail, and once abroad they had little contact with those they had left behind. They were isolated in a different culture and most of them stayed, with only infrequent visits home, until illness, old age or death released them. The risks to health could be greater in the mission field even than in nineteenth century Britain, and the news from the outposts was sometimes heartbreaking. In 1894 John E. Woodstock arrived from England at Matadi on the Congo river. He was expecting to move further up-river and begin the missionary work he had been trained for, but

Chapter 8

before he could even begin the journey he succumbed to sickness and just weeks after his arrival he died.

And there were other risks. The nations of the world did not always appreciate what they saw as Britain's interference in their affairs. In China particularly there was a long history of resentment against foreigners. At the end of the century the political situation there was unstable, and in 1900 bands of rebels from a society known in the West as the Boxers began to roam the countryside attacking missionaries, who they felt were subverting traditional Chinese beliefs and culture. One of their first targets was the mission at T'ai-Yüan Fu. The attack was ferocious. The mission buildings were burned to the ground, and all forty-four of the missionaries and children living there were killed. The Edwards family were away in England at the time and so escaped, but George Stokes is reported to have been beaten to death and Margaret, the woman he had met and married there, was tied to an ox cart by her hair and dragged along the ground until she died.

The news was brought back to the church at Salem, and must have caused deep shock among the people who had known George since childhood and had accepted Margaret, sight unseen, as a member when they were married. But they wrote in a memorandum to the families of the two martyrs, 'We as a Church desire to acknowlege our humble submission to the All-wise Will of our Father in heaven . . . This Church also prays and believes that great good will accrue to the Kingdom of God in China and at home by reason of this heavy affliction.' Still to be seen in the wall of the corridor at Salem are the memorial plaques to John Woodstock and to George and Margaret Stokes, who had made the ultimate sacrifice in the service of their Lord.

Interest in missionary work bred missionaries. Knowing the missionaries personally bred further interest. This continued into the twentieth century, and more of the young men and women who began their evangelistic training in the villages around Dover went on to serve in more distant places. In 1920 Hilda Bradley went to India, and in 1921 Elsie Brookes, in 1931 Leslie Taylor, and in 1933 Kathleen Harvey (who later became Mrs Taylor) went to the Congo. The annual weekend when BMS missionaries home on furlough came to tell of their work continued, and a variety of other meetings were

136

Roll of Honour.

MISSIONARIES, MINISTERS, AND SIMILAR WORKERS who have been or are associated with our Church in one or more of these ways, namely,—as Sunday Scholars (S), or as Teachers (T), or as Members (M).

Hunt, Edward.—(M.) Missionary to China, 1889-1922. Joined Salem 1906. Deceased 1922.

Hunt, Alice (née Whitford).—(M.) Missionary to China, 1890-1921. Joined Salem 1906. Deceased 1921.

Stokes, Geo. Wm.—(S.T.M.) Missionary to China, 1891-1900. Martyred 1900.

Stokes, Margaret Ingram (née Whitaker).—(M,) Missionary to China, 1892-1900. Joined Salem 1898. Martyred 1900.

Macdonald, Mary Harriet Ann.—(S.M.) Missionary to India, 1894—19'

Woodcock, John E.—(T.M.) Missionary to Congoland, Africa 1894. Deceased 1894.

Jarry (M.B.E.), Frederick Wm.—(S.T.M.) Missionary to India, 1895—19'

Jarry, Agnes Burns (née Moodie).—(S.M.) Missionary to India, 1897—19'

Moodie, Helen (now Mrs. Skeen).—(S,M.) Missionary to Ceylon, 1896-1904.

Burnett, Christopher.—(T.) Minister in Canada and U.S.A., 1897—19'

Hicks, Geo. Edward—(S.T.M.) Missionary to India, 1899—19'

Hicks, Eva Grey (née Gibson).—(T.M.) Missionary to India, 1902—19'

Ferguson, Mary Rose.—(S.) Missionary to China, 1904-1919.

Brooks, Elsie Winifred.—(M.) Evangelist in Scotland (1912-1917), Missionary to Congoland, Africa, 1922. Deceased 1922.

Bradley (M.A.) Wilfred Scott.—(M.) Minister in England, 1914-1918. Deceased 1918.

Barling, Frank Sidney.—(S.T.M.) Missionary to China, 1915—19'

Blackett, George Milton.—(S.T.M.) Minister in Canada, 1915—19'

Bradley, Hilda Ruth—(T.M.) Missionary to India, 1920—19'

Barling, Stanley Nelson.—(S.T.M.) Finance Secretary to the National Council of Y.M.C.A. for India, Burma, and Ceylon, 1921—19'

Bradley (B.A.) Margaret Sarah (S.T.M.) Assistant Minister in England, 1921—19'

Those whose names are marked —19' are still serving in the spheres indicated.

Roll of Honour printed in 1922

Chapter 8

held in the evenings during the year – in 1927, for instance, there were talks by the Leper Mission and the British and Foreign Bible Society and a well-attended film lecture about 'The Great Congo'.

But the world situation was changing. By the end of the first world war Britain was beginning to lose its supremacy over vast tracts of the globe. The nations were starting to rebel against its paternalistic government and demand freedom to run their own affairs, and missionary as well as commercial and political institutions had to alter. As the century progressed Western missionaries began to acknowledge that the task of evangelism could be done equally well or even better by local Christians, and in many cases they handed over to them entirely and confined themselves to work in medicine and engineering, personal evangelism, and an advisory or training role in church life where needed. At home, too, the church was changing. Walter Holyoak retired and Stanley Tweed took over, and the old, stern call to duty and sacrifice was muted. After 1933 no more missionaries left from Salem for thirty years.

The church did not forget its responsibilities, though. Compared with many churches, Salem always gave generously to work overseas. People took missionary boxes home to put by regular small sums – in 1949 seventy people out of a membership of two hundred and forty were using them – and the box-opening meeting, with a talk and refreshments, was an annual ceremony for many years. There were garden parties in the grounds of St Margaret's chapel in aid of the BMS, and meetings with speakers and fund-raising for other causes. In 1953 the 'small woman', Gladys Aylward, came to speak at one of these; Salem people found that she was indeed a small person but dynamic. She spoke for three hours and was remembered for fifty years. Door-to-door collecting for Christian Aid began in Dover in 1966 and Salem has responded for many years under Joyce Pocknall's faithful, unobtrusive co-ordination.

The next missionaries associated with Salem did not leave directly from Dover. In 1961 Roy Connor had left Salem to train at Spurgeon's College for the ministry. By this time missionary work was often a short period out of the middle of a lifetime, and he was minister at Fareham when in 1977 he and his wife Margaret heard the call to the mission field and left for Brazil.

Prayer card sent out to friends by Roy and Margaret Connor

They would be returning eventually to another house in England so they did not want to get rid of their furniture, so as well as giving money the church at Salem stored the furniture for them in the empty top floor of the manse at 248 Folkestone Road. In 1981 Roy came to Salem as the speaker on missionary Sunday. They stayed in Brazil for seven years and then returned to a pastorate in Bognor Regis.

The last missionaries to go out from Salem were five people who moved to Dover for a few years and left for mission work from here. In 1962 Gloria Guest, a teacher, went from Salem to St Colm's College, Edinburgh and from there to work in East Pakistan. Chris and Heather Jealous went in 1977 to work with the Christian Literature Crusade in Hampshire, and a few years later Chris Holcombe and his wife Sue went out to work in an African hospital. Individual members supported them with prayer and gifts and letters, but they had been part of the church for such a few years that the church somehow did not feel the tie with them that they had with the missionaries of fifty years before. More recently missionary societies, recognising that people find it easier to relate to individuals than to an impersonal organisation, have introduced link schemes. Two missionary couples, John and Brenda Hart with Latin Link in Ecuador and Bob and Ruth Ellett with the BMS in Nepal, are now 'our' missionaries, and regular letters and visits from them mean the church is familiar with their activities and understands better how to give and pray.

Chapter 8

In England during the twentieth century interest in spiritual things has waned. The slaughter of two world wars raised difficult questions, universal education encouraged people to question traditional beliefs, and increases in the standard of living made this world a more attractive option. Nonetheless the command to go and tell has never been revoked, and the church is still called to evangelise. At different times this has been done in different ways. In the fifties the American evangelist Billy Graham came to Britain and drew thousands to his 'crusade' meetings in the stadium at Harringay. A special train was run from East Kent to London for the event in 1954, and the following year radio links were set up so that the churches in Dover, like many all over the country, could hear the message at a distance. But one of the first attempts to present the old message in a new format was the Billy Graham film, 'Souls in Conflict'. Islwyn Evans was instrumental in arranging the showing which had such dramatic results in Dover. Later evangelism at Salem focussed on lower-key activities, such as 'Good News down the Street', which involved visitation to the houses in the neighbourhood or to people on the fringe of the fellowship.

But in 1991 the churches of Dover raised their profile again when they banded together, under the lead of the 'Christians Together in Dover' chairman, Alan Simper, to organise 'Tell Dover', a week-long mission that took place in a marquee in Pencester Gardens. There were children's activities each afternoon, meetings in the evenings with speakers ranging from the Archbishop of Canterbury to Salem's own Geoff Cook, and people on hand during the day for individual counselling or conversation. How far it reached its objective of telling the town the good news is difficult to say. There were few if any stories of immediate conversions. All the meetings were well-attended, but it has to be said that a large proportion of those who came to them were those already involved in church life. The comment might have been made, as it was of a mission a hundred years earlier in Dover, that it 'brought much blessing to believers, but we have not seen as yet the results in the conversion of the unsaved which we had prayed and looked for.' Perhaps for such an event to be truly effective the impetus has to come from within the churches and not just from a small group of enthusiastic leaders. All the same it was a tremendous combined effort, and it resulted not least in the revival and encouragement of the churches themselves and closer links between them.

The last activity that David Howells introduced at Salem before he left, an activity he could not stay to see put into operation, was the running of an Alpha course. This again is an attempt to use modern technology to reach the modern world. The West today is used to television bringing high-quality information and entertainment into its own homes, and the Alpha course, developed at Holy Trinity Church, Brompton, uses the video recorder to do the same for the gospel. It is simply a series of talks on video, but it is well-designed and is offered as a whole package with the Alpha team's commercial-style marketing and precise instructions for its effective presentation, including a welcome meal. It was used at Salem on Sunday afternoons for thirteen weeks of the autumn of 1998. A large proportion of the church was involved in its organisation, and more than thirty visitors came, of whom about a quarter did not regularly attend any church. On a questionnaire given out at the end, eighteen visitors said they had made new friends during the course, ten had learnt new and helpful things about Christianity, eleven felt they had moved closer to God and a few, who had considered themselves Christians before, had now committed themselves more deeply. The vivid re-statement of Christian beliefs clearly brought the gospel to life for many both inside and outside the church, and a number of those from outside continued to come to worship on Sunday evenings after the course was finished.

Once again in 2001 the church is using the video to reach people, this time in their own homes. Ten churches are working together to take the 'Jesus video' out to three thousand houses in and around Dover in the summer of 2001. This video has been made to show people – many of whom will have had no church background and very little Christian teaching from school – the dramatised story of Jesus' life, death and resurrection. Then there will be follow-up at the individual churches for any whose interest is caught.

The church is wise to move with the times. The gospel has not changed, but perhaps not very many in today's sophisticated society are likely to be attracted to an evangelistic rally to hear even a celebrated preacher. Film and

CHAPTER 8

The changing face of the church magazine

video require less initial commitment from their viewers, and resources can be put into high-quality presentation that would not be possible for small missions run by local people.

But in the end the success of all evangelism depends on the quality of the church's own Christian life. People may be reached by missions or video presentations or house-to-house visitation, or they may be brought to church by friends or neighbours, or they may find their own way in because they become aware of a need in their life and hope that the church can fill it. Whatever the original stimulus, the enquirer, having once been brought within the sound of the gospel, must find a real and living faith in those who proclaim it; otherwise after a short time he will dismiss the church and the church's God as, in the Alpha phrase, boring, untrue and irrelevant, and simply leave again. It is for us not just to preach but to live the gospel.

CHAPTER 9
Past and Future

NO-ONE knows why, when the chapel in Biggin Street was built in 1840, it was given the name Salem. At that time it couldn't, of course, simply have been called Dover Baptist Church; it needed a name to distinguish it from Pentside, Dover, and later from Dover Tabernacle and two other short-lived Baptist causes in the town. But why Salem, nobody knows. Nonconformist chapels were often called by Biblical names, and there was a Salem chapel for a time in Folkestone and another at St Peter's, Broadstairs. The minister from Salem, St Peter's, J. M. Cramp, was one of those who came to help the church through its break from Pentside, and Berkeley Johnson, in his unpublished notes on the church's history, suggests that the Dover Salem may have been called after the St Peter's Salem as a compliment to him. As far as anyone knows there was never any connection with Salem, Massachusetts, of infamous story – or with any other Salem in the U.S.A.

The word 'Salem' is a shortened form of Jerusalem, and the new church may well have felt that the name of the celestial city, the new Jerusalem, was a very appropriate one for a church's home. But the meaning of the word itself is 'peace', and perhaps when they chose the name they were remembering the bitterness and recrimination among the members of Pentside and hoping that from now on the new church in its new building would be able to live in peace.

Originally the name was given to the chapel itself and not to the people who worshipped there. As late as 1884 the church was referring to itself as 'the church of Christ assembling at Salem chapel, Dover'. But gradually, by a natural shorthand, the name came to mean the people as well as the building, and by 1923 Walter Holyoak was telling St Margaret's that 'Salem had kept their promise of giving £1 for every £10 raised by this church' (for decorating). Since technically some of the St Margaret's congregation were themselves members of Salem Baptist Church this may have been illogical, but everyone understood that Salem meant the people at Biggin Street, and the people of the chapels were called by the names of their villages.

By the beginning of the first world war all the other Baptist churches in Dover had closed. (Pentside, by then meeting in Queen Street, was the last in 1909, and some of their members came to worship at Salem.) There was no real need any more for a distinguishing name for the church in Biggin Street, and after a while it began to seem that the name might be changed to the more general and easily identified 'Dover Baptist Church'. Letters and

Wedding of Alison Wheeler and Tom Ruddle 2001 [photo June Booth]

Chapter 9

documents between 1945 and 1951 are headed 'Dover (Salem) Baptist Church'; the name reverted for a while to 'Salem Baptist' and then changed again in 1996 to 'Dover Baptist Church (Salem)'. But no-one has really wanted to abandon 'Salem' altogether. It would be a pity to lose the covering banner of peace.

Looking back over the century and a half of the church's history it may not at first be obvious that it has lived at peace either within itself or with its neighbours. There have been differences of opinion with the local association. There have been times when member has been divided against member, deacon against minister, member against moderator, deacon against deacon. There have been stormy church meetings, letters to the press, divisions and revisions and resignations. Where in all this is God's peace?

Partly the disputes must have been the work of Satan, who stirs up dissension in the church when he can to make it that much less effective. But perhaps it is also true that to expect total calm and agreement in any organisation is to expect stagnation. The peace God gives to his obedient church is not the peace of a land-locked water, still because it is going nowhere. It is more like the smooth, steady movement of a fast-flowing stream. Over the years there have in fact been long periods when the church has been at peace, and generally speaking those have been the times when the members have been directed by a strong minister, inspired by prayer and the Holy Spirit, and working together for the extension of the kingdom.

Now we have finally ceased to call ourselves Salem: we have become simply Dover Baptist Church – though we keep the old name over the door. As we go forward through the twenty-first century, perhaps we should not expect perfect calm among us. Certainly we do not want to become a church that agrees in everything and achieves nothing. In the future as in the past there will probably be differences of opinion between members, but we trust that they will be only the swirls and eddies on the surface that say that underneath the current is running deep.

The church has lived and worked at Salem for more than a hundred and fifty years, worshipping God, loving its neighbours, and proclaiming the message of Jesus Christ and his salvation to all who will hear. We pray that it

Past and Future

may continue to do so for many years to come. And as people look at us, both now and in the future, we pray that they may see the likeness of God reflected in us, and that when they come to join us they may feel in our company something of his peace.

Dover Baptist Church Family collage 2001 [photo June Booth]

APPENDIX
Church Statistics

MEMBERSHIP

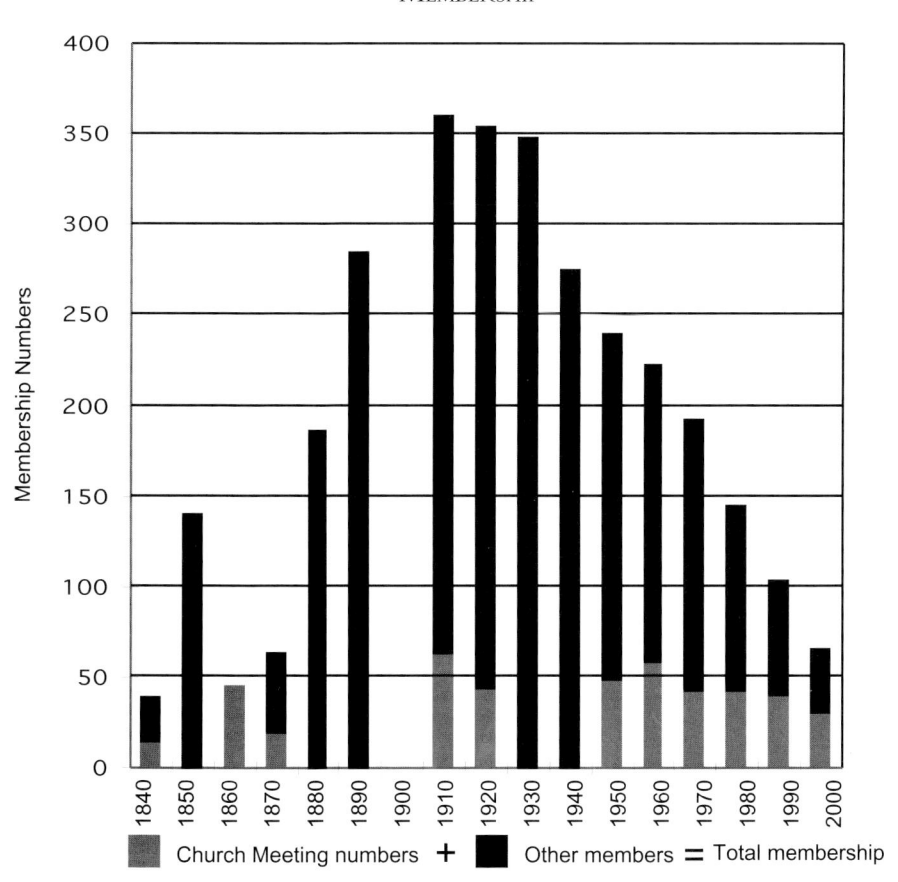

APPENDIX

SUNDAY SCHOOL

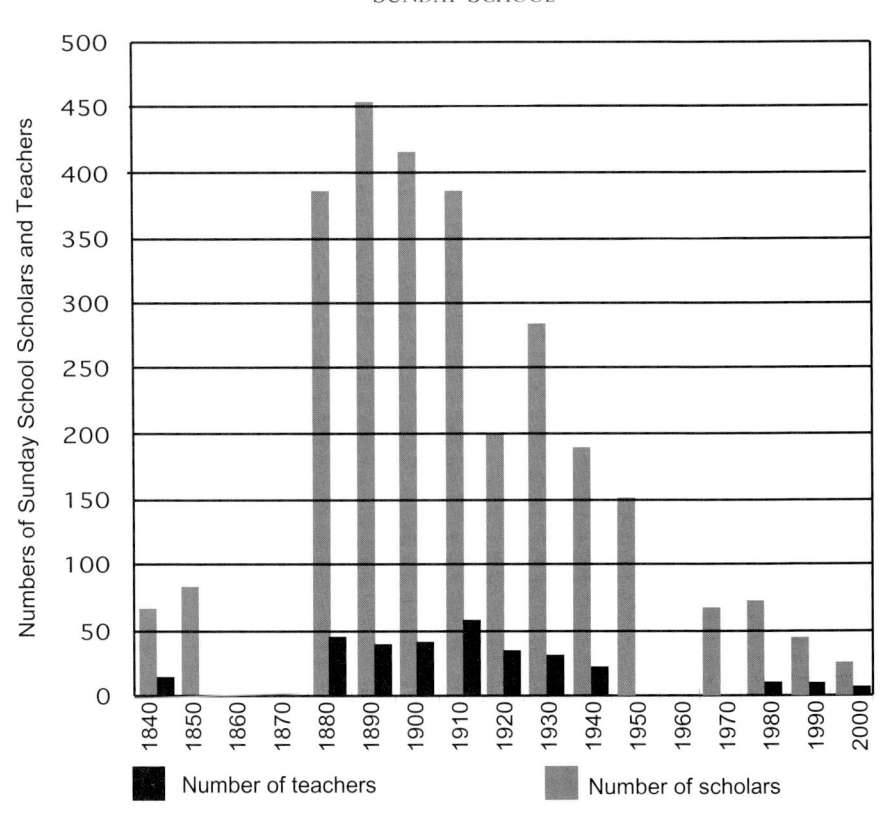

Church Statistics

Actual figures on which histograms based

	Membership numbers	Church Meeting numbers	Sunday School Scholars	Sunday School Teachers
1840	39	14	65	14
1850	140★		80★	
1860		45		
1870	63¶	19§		
1880	186		385	45
1890	285		451	38
1900			437	40
1910	360	63†	387	56
1920	354	44	197‡	31‡
1930	348		282	30
1940	275		185#	22#
1950	239	49	150★★	
1960	223	58		
1970	192	42	64	
1980	147	42	70	8
1990	103	40	45	9
2000	66	30	23	6

★ statistics for 1849   ¶ statistics for 1871   § statistics for January 1872
† statistics for AGM   ‡ statistics for 1919   # statistics for 1939
★★ statistics for 1949

Church meeting figures are for an ordinary (not Annual or Special) church meeting, including deacons, in the year in question or the nearest year for which there are figures

Sunday School figures do not include totals for the mission Sunday Schools

Bibliography

Batcheller, W. 1844. *The New Dover Guide.* Dover (6th edition)

Buffard, Frank. 1963. *Kent and Sussex Baptist Associations*

Burnett, John. 1979. *Plenty and Want.* Scolar Press

Chadwick, Owen. *The Victorian Church, vols 1 & 2.* A & C Black, 1970, 1971

Clark, W. Philip, *Eythorne: Our Baptist Heritage.* Thanet, n.d.

Cliff, Philip B. 1986. *The Rise and Development of the Sunday School Movement in England 1780–1980.* Redhill; National Christian Education Council

Fishman, William J. 1988. *East End 1888.* Duckworth

Gray, Adrian. 1984. *The London, Chatham and Dover Railway.* Meresborough Books

Harrison, Brian. 1971. *Drink and the Victorians.* Faber & Faber

Hayden, Roger. 1990. *English Baptist History and Heritage.* Baptist Union of Great Britain

Holyoak, Walter. 1914. *Dover Baptists.* Dover

Humphreys, Roy S. 1993. *Dover at War 1939–45.* Sutton

Leach, Derek. 1999. *The Life and Times of a Dovorian, Lilian Kay.* Riverdale Publications.

Johnson, Berkeley John. Unpublished notes on the history of Salem

Bibliography

Jones, John Bavington. 1938 (edn). *Annals of Dover.* Dover

Jones, John Bavington. 1907. *Dover: A Perambulation of the Town. Port and Fortress.* Dover

Miller. 1924. *Eythorne, the story of a village Baptist Church.* Baptist Union Publications

Rudkin, Mabel S. 1933. *Inside Dover 1914–1918.* Elliott Stock

Springhall, Fraser & Hoare. 1983. *A History of the Boys' Brigade 1883–1983.* Collins

Stanley, Brian. 1992. *The History of the Baptist Missionary Society.* T & T Clark

Stocks, Ronald. 1975. *The Control of Pounds and Pints.* Buckland

Thompson, F. M. L. 1988. *The Rise of Respectable Society.* Fontana paperback

Yates, Hume and Hastings. 1994. *Religion & Society in Kent 1640–1914.* Boydell Press

Salem records including minutes of church meetings, deacons' meetings, Sunday School meetings and chapel communicants' conferences

Index

Alpha Course, 141
Anabaptists, 11

Band of Hope, 115–116, 128
Baptism, 66–67, 83
Baptist Missionary Society, 32, 132–133, 139
Baptist Union, 41, 45, 79, 91, 93
Baptists, General/Particular, 11–12
Bayly, Leonard, 45–48
Biggin Street chapel, 18–19, 54, 66–76
Billy Graham rallies, 140
    film, 50, 140
Booth, Nigel, 62–63
Bosworth, Frederic, 23–26
Boys (Life) Brigade, 116, 118–119
Burial ground, Salem, 68–70

Capel chapel, 100–108
Choir, 88–89
Christian Endeavour, 115
Christians Together in Dover, 94, 140
Church meeting, 84–86
Colporteurs, 97–98

Communion, 89–91
    open/closed, 14, 18
Connor, Roy, 50, 109, 138–139

Deacons, 80–83
Dorcas Society, 32, 127
Dover town, 64–66, 70, 75
Dover Free Church Council, 53, 94

Edwards, Ebenezer, 35, 133–136
Edwards, Elijah, 33–37, 128, 132–134
Edwards Road, 75
Evans, Islwyn, 49–52, 118, 140
Ewell Minnis chapel, 39, 96–104, 133
Eythorne Baptist church, 13

Fector, Caroline, 96–97

Girls (Life) Brigade, 116–119

Hewlett, James, 17–22
Holyoak, Walter, 37–42, 128
Hopper, John, 50, 62
Howells, David, 60–61, 141
Hymn-singing, 87–88

INDEX

Ibberson, Alfred, 28–32

Johnson, Berkeley 52–55, 144

Kent (& Sussex) Baptist Association, 91–92
Kingsford, Alfred, 22, 26, 27, 29, 31–32

Local preachers, 100, 103
Luther, Martin, 10
Maison Dieu Road chapel, 54–55, 76–79
Maternity box, 127
Missionaries from Salem, 134–139

National Sunday School Union, 111, 112
  centenary celebrations, 111
Norkett, David, 57–58

Passingham, Robert Townsend, 31–33, 80, 81, 132–133
Pennells, Ernest, 56–57, 85 86
Pentside church, 14–15, 144–145
Pepper, William, 22
Pew rents, 28
Pitt, Alexander, 27–28

Reformation, 11–12, 86–87, 89–90
Routley, Graham, 58–59

St Margaret's chapel, 96–106, 133, 145
'Salem', origin and meaning, 144
Sermon, 86–87
Skinner, Frederick, 36–37
Soup run, 123–124
Spurgeon, Charles Haddon, 33, 35
Stokes, George, 36, 134–136
Sunday School, 18, 38–40, 43, 45, 109–114, 119–121

Tavenor, Samuel, 12–13
'Tell Dover' mission, 60, 140–141
Temperance movement, 128
Temple Ewell chapel, 60, 95–108, 133
Tract Distribution Society, 131–132
Tweed, Stanley, 42–44

War, 1914–1918, 40–41, 126
  1939–1945, 44–46, 126
Woodstock, John E., 135–136

Youth clubs, 118–119